Reading *Loving De
reading *Traveling* o
something to be sa
Deliberately is a lot l ... chocolates
from a big box. Just take one or two pieces at a time, slowly and completely enjoying what each (very different from all the rest) has to offer. Candy for the heart and the head.

༄

One of the best things about reading *Loving Deliberately* for me was how it challenged me to consider what loving deliberately is all about and to think about who and what I love deliberately in *my* life. Thanks for the book as well as the challenge, Steve!

༄

Now the series is complete. And I couldn't have thought of three better subjects: traveling, aging, and loving all deliberately. This third book is a change of pace, but it works so very well. Also, I thoroughly enjoy Steve's conversational writing style and his choice and arrangement of the selections that make up his anthology.

༄

At the suggestion of a friend, I read Studs Terkel's book, *Working*, about thirty years ago. I thoroughly enjoyed it, so I can certainly understand why Steve thought it might be a good model to follow albeit in a loose way. In any case, it's too bad that Mr. Terkel is no longer around to read *Loving Deliberately* because I feel certain that he would have had a great appreciation for what Steve has accomplished here.

☙

This is such a wonderful anthology from such a wide variety of people and experiences and from so many places and times. I have my favorites as I am sure that anyone who reads this book will have. But I must say that the beautiful and haunting love letter from Major Sullivan Ballou to his wife, Sarah, is special - extraordinarily so, for me. Thanks, Steve, for introducing me to this incredibly moving piece of writing as well as so many others in your collection.

☙

Another treat for the eyes and the mind, *Loving Deliberately* is a perfect third and final piece of the *Deliberately* series. Thank you for what you have done, Steve. You have given each of your readers something to think about and, yes, to treasure.

Loving *Deliberately*

An Eclectic Anthology of Reflections on the Subject

Edited by Steve Bannow

Copyright © 2019 Edited by Steve Bannow.

All rights reserved. No part of this book may be used or reproduced by any means, graphic, electronic, or mechanical, including photocopying, recording, taping or by any information storage retrieval system without the written permission of the author except in the case of brief quotations embodied in critical articles and reviews.

This book is a work of non-fiction. Unless otherwise noted, the author and the publisher make no explicit guarantees as to the accuracy of the information contained in this book and in some cases, names of people and places have been altered to protect their privacy.

Archway Publishing books may be ordered through booksellers or by contacting:

Archway Publishing
1663 Liberty Drive
Bloomington, IN 47403
www.archwaypublishing.com
1 (888) 242-5904

Because of the dynamic nature of the Internet, any web addresses or links contained in this book may have changed since publication and may no longer be valid. The views expressed in this work are solely those of the author and do not necessarily reflect the views of the publisher, and the publisher hereby disclaims any responsibility for them.

Any people depicted in stock imagery provided by Getty Images are models, and such images are being used for illustrative purposes only. Certain stock imagery © Getty Images.

ISBN: 978-1-4808-7562-3 (sc)
ISBN: 978-1-4808-7561-6 (e)

Library of Congress Control Number: 2019904935

Print information available on the last page.

Archway Publishing rev. date: 5/8/2019

"I went to the woods because I wished to live deliberately, to front only the essential facts of life, and see if I could not learn what it had to teach, and not, when I came to die, discover that I had not lived."

Henry David Thoreau
From *Walden: or, Life in the Woods*

For Barbara
And
Daniel

☙

Preface

This is the third and final book in my *Deliberately* series. The idea of collecting the thoughts about the meaning of something vitally important to the human experience from lots of folks – many of whom I have never met – came to me a few years ago. The plan was inspired by Studs Terkel and his important book: *Working*. If you have been fortunate enough to have read Studs' book, you know that it is a brilliant collection of comments from people from all walks of life who agreed to share their thoughts on what work/working *means* to them. So, in taking the idea of collecting and reporting the comments that a wide variety of individuals have about another extraordinarily important part of life, I am more than a bit of a thief. Somehow I don't think that Studs would mind. And, by the way, those who submitted their reflections to this anthology had a much more difficult task than those who shared their thoughts on working. You see, Studs *recorded* his contributors; those who contributed to *Loving Deliberately* did so in *writing*. I will have more to say about this important distinction later.

As for my decision to make *loving* deliberately my subject, that thought arose indirectly out of my overall plan for this series and was a much more recent event. Acting as editor rather than sole proprietor of this anthology's contents was a no-brainer. I cannot even scratch the surface of my topic – especially since it is so utterly subjective and experience-driven. So, I am much more the conductor on this journey-train than I am the engineer. As you will soon see, the substance of this book comes from the thoughts, dreams, desires, and life events of scores of folks – of different ages, from different places in the world and in time. These writers offer an amazing array of perspectives; yet each is similar to his or her fellow contributors in their shared human-ness.

I also made a determination at the outset to do virtually no editing of the written words of those who chose to participate in this project other than to arrange the pieces in a way that, I hope, will make some thematic sense. I wanted to give folks the chance to have free reign to take on this tough assignment without having to worry about grammatical finesse, punctuation niceties, or even spelling for that matter.* Some of the writing will be raw, untamed, perhaps. But, if the meaning, the unique idea behind the writing comes shining through, I will simply leave it alone. I promise you and have promised my contributors that this will always be the case. Moreover, as of this moment, I can't even say who will contribute or just how diverse this group of contributors and contributions may be. In fact, I can't tell you much, if anything, about what specifically is ahead in these pages because I am writing this preface before having read even one of the dozen or so contributions that I have received so far. I am sharing some of my aspirations about *Loving Deliberately* here without anything concrete to go on. It just seems like the right way to go.

As you might imagine, I am excited about the possibilities

---

* You may be interested to have a look at the information sheet that I provided to everyone who indicated to me that they would be interested in submitting something for inclusion in the book. I have included it as an Appendix.

for this anthology, this collection of written responses to the question: *What does loving deliberately mean to you?* I am hopeful that what will end up filling these pages will be dozens and dozens of truly unique reflections related in dozens and dozens of different ways. I am aware that some folks will go through the significant thinking process, the soul-searching, and the introspection to develop their own notions of the meaning and importance of loving deliberately but will stop short of actually submitting what – if anything – they came up with. That is perfectly fine with me. And I am also hopeful that everyone who reflects on this question – and this goes for our contributors as well as those of you who are involved in this project as readers only – will learn and grow as I certainly have.

SWB March 2016

༄

A Preface *post scriptum*

Over two and a half years after I wrote the Preface to this book, I began the challenge of organizing and arranging the offerings that I had collected. I feel that this process is important because each *piece* is important and deserving of careful consideration in terms of where and how it is presented. After much thought and several experiments, I decided to group the pieces thematically. As you will quickly discover, there is no symmetry in the number of offerings per part. A few actually contain most of the pieces; while a couple only have two or three. Some decisions about where to place certain selections within the six parts of this anthology were very easy – the only challenge being where within a group to place them. But other decisions on thematic location were very difficult because some pieces straddled thematic lines and others simply defied categorization. So ... in some cases, I just went with my gut. The point that I wish to make here is that you may wonder why certain pieces are placed where they are; you may even think that mistakes were made by me in the process. If this is the case, *good*. This would show that you care enough to take a stand on the issue. If you see nothing odd in my arrangement decisions, that is fine, as well. In any case, be assured that my decision-making process regarding group/part titles and the actual arrangement of the selections herein were made ... *deliberately.*

Oh yes, and speaking of this anthology's organization ... about a month ago, I awoke from a dream about *Loving Deliberately* with a must-do idea: I absolutely *had* to include a now-famous letter that is one of the most perfect expressions of loving deliberately that I have ever encountered. I am referring to the pre-Battle of Bull Run letter from Major Sullivan Ballou to his wife, Sarah. It is found on pages 121-123. I have nothing more to say about Major Ballou's letter for now, except that I know that it will make a very positive and lasting impression upon you – if it hasn't already. Once I decided to add this letter to the book, it became clear to me that I should include other works by important people whom I have never met and never will meet. It was not *their* choice to contribute their work to this anthology. It was *mine*. I know that you and I could debate the choices of this particular assortment of offerings that I have included, and I invite you to consider which ones you would have left out and what pieces you would have added. In any case, what I hope you do when you consider these pieces is to reflect on why they are included at all. Why/how are they dealing with loving deliberately? Perhaps these writers are very much like the others whose very act of creating something (a poem, a letter, a slice of life) is an unquestionably real and meaningful demonstration of love – *acting* on their love … in other words, loving *deliberately*. This collection of twenty pieces is distributed throughout the anthology – each placed within the part of the book that I felt was most appropriate.

And now it is time to get to the heart of the matter.

SWB November 2018

༒

A Preface *post post scriptum*

It is December 17, 2018, and I am just a week or two away from sending the manuscript of *Loving Deliberately* to my publisher. I cannot do this, however, until I tell you about some very recent events that somehow have had an important place in the completion of this book.

On the fourth of this month, we received word that my life partner, Barbara, lost her son and only child. This was devastating news that we will be dealing with one day, one hour, one moment at a time ….

Miraculously, two days after Dan's death, his Love, Kelli, found a piece that Dan had written but had not yet sent to me for inclusion in the anthology. Of course, I found a fitting place for it, although it is not identifiable by (Dan's) name. While performing the eulogy at Dan's memorial service and preparing to share with the guests what he had written about loving deliberately, I began to preface what I was about to read by referring to the "wonder," the "miracle" of having Dan's piece find its way to his mother and me through Kelli. And just as I was relating those exact words to describe the fortuitous finding of Dan's reflections, the microphone seemed to leap from the lectern. I caught it in mid-air. It had not been balancing precariously on the edge; nor had I come into contact with it. Hundreds of guests observed this occurrence. The leaping microphone was certainly a show stopper, but I was able to gather myself, comment briefly (with at an attempt at some mild humor), and continue with the eulogy. My belief system as it pertains to the spiritual world left me with no explanation immediately after the leaping microphone episode, nor do I have one now, and I am content with the probability that I never will. There were others present (and there are others who were not there) however, who don't merely think … they *know* what happened: Dan – in his typical prankster mode – had and took his chance at having his moment. In any case… Miraculous.

This morning I received word that one of my dearest Friends, Jami, died yesterday. We first met in fifth grade. I knew that she had been ill but was shocked by the suddenness of her passing. After informing Barbara of our loss and touching base with Jami's cousin, Peggy, I knew that I needed to inform my sister, Elissa, of what had happened. Realizing that I had left my phone in the car, I went out to the garage to retrieve it. Upon doing so, I saw that I had received a text message. The text information that accompanied it stated that it was from my sister. When I opened the text, there was no written message. But there was a photo – one of the very last and very best photos of … perhaps you can guess who … Jami and me. My first thought was that my sister had somehow managed to find a copy of the photo and had sent it to me as a loving way to let me know that she had heard the news.

When I called Elissa, I learned that she had *not*, in fact, sent me the photo. Its origin as an image in my text messages is – and, in all likelihood, will forever remain – another wonderful mystery to me. It is no mystery, however, to many others who are fortunate enough to have an abiding, unyielding belief in the wonderful presence of spiritual beings. In any case, once again … Miraculous.

I think that you can understand why I felt it important, necessary to relate these happenings to you. Each of us comes to the matter of loving deliberately as a result of our own experiences. I am certain that the events that I have recently experienced and have just related add an entirely new dimension and a wholly different texture and timbre to what you are about to read and reflect upon in the pages that follow. Thank you for letting me share my accounts of these wondrous, miraculous events with you. I wish you well.

SWB December 2018

Contents

Introduction xix

PART 1 Defining Loving Deliberately ... Deliberately 1
PART 2 Loving Others ... Deliberately 63
PART 3 Loving a Place ... Deliberately 101
PART 4 Loving Work ... Deliberately 109
PART 5 Loving One's Country ... Deliberately 119
PART 6 Loving an Idea ... Deliberately 127

Conclusion 135
Appendix 137

Introduction

As I mentioned in the Preface, this is the third and last book of my *Deliberately* series. You may also be aware that I owe the theme of traveling, aging, and loving *deliberately* to Henry David Thoreau. A key passage from his *Walden* is at the heart, the soul of each of my first three books. It bears repeating here and you will see it – actually a longer rendition – later in this anthology:

> I went to the woods because I wished to live deliberately, to front only the essential facts of life, and see if I could not learn what it had to teach, and not, when I came to die, discover that I had not lived.

My purpose in writing each of these books has been to make an attempt to get at the essence of three of the most interesting if not the most important aspects of life for us human animals. Since loving deliberately is, by far, the most difficult of these things for me to get my head and heart around, I decided to cheat ... a lot. I received the help of some folks I know and others whom I do not know to help me out. The writings in this collection that I have gathered and read carefully have confirmed several things that I believed before I even started this project in the winter of 2016. Most of us do have similar ways of defining or describing *love* and *loving*. I think that most of us could agree that defining love as a feeling of significant fondness or affection for someone or something would be an acceptable way to relate its meaning – at least for starters. But most of us *feel* and/or *experience* love in ways that vary profoundly in their uniqueness as much as we, as individuals, do. Love is, after all, an essentially subjective thing. And I think we could also agree that love is not the same thing as lov*ing*. I may love someone but putting that love into action by *loving* that person is a more complicated matter. And then we add the "deliberately" part. Doing so raises the stakes. To do something deliberately is to act upon/with purpose, to be focussed on the act, to be engaged, mindful. But, as is the case with love and loving, how this actually plays out in the experience of each of us is often as different as we are from one another. Yet the commonality of the loving experience is archetypal, and our shared human-ness cannot be denied.

So … an entire book devoted to explore what a simple two-word phrase means to scores of people from all over the place throughout many, many years…? Sure. After all, what is more important and fascinating than the topic of love, in general, and, perhaps, loving deliberately, in particular?

For me, loving deliberately must be discovered over time and in stages. Getting there requires a true desire to do so. It requires experience, learning, and growth. And, I sincerely believe, it requires the essential ingredient of *Self*-love. This discovery was relatively slow in coming for me, just as Self-love itself was something that came to me relatively late in my life. In my younger days, I was not aware of its meaning or importance; it was certainly not in my nature; its importance and relevance were, for me, acquired tastes. The process required plenty of pain for me and, unfortunately, for others as well. Some folks are more ... able or enlightened or ... lucky. For them, grasping and experiencing the essence of Self-love came much sooner and often with much less pain than it did for me. I do not believe that their Self-love is any less important or precious than mine just because they did not have to live as long or travel as far as I did to find it. It is what it is and we know it when we have it.

The next necessary step in the loving deliberately process is to determine what we do with Self-love once we have it. Do we use it as a springboard to loving deliberately? My hope has been to answer that question by reading what others have to say on the matter – realizing that not everyone who is willing to comment on loving deliberately has learned and practiced Self-love as a base for it.

I do not believe that loving deliberately requires a steady level of awareness or intensity. It can manifest itself in as mellow a manner as simply knowing the degree and depth of your affection for a living being or a thing. Or it can be felt and expressed in as passionate and even agitated a way as to be almost frightening in its energy. While I have fathered no children, I have come to the conclusion that rearing children often involves many good examples of both the mellowness and the intensity associated with loving deliberately. But loving deliberately is certainly not strictly a parent/child condition. It is or at least *can* be something essential, rudimentary in any meaningful relationship. And another thing: **Loving deliberately must be for keeps.** Please don't confuse this with loving unconditionally. There are very important differences between the two for me even though I know that, for others, they are almost the same. You see, it is the Self-love part and the trust in what, consequently, I can perceive about my feelings about those whom I love that keeps me especially connected, focussed on the importance of loving others – and, most important, my Self – *deliberately*. This requires patience, trust, passion, and tolerance. But it also takes courage … the courage to leave negative, hurtful relationships that I trust myself well enough to know cannot be repaired or the courage to walk away from destructive people to whom my Self-love has enabled me to say "Good-bye … for Good."

As I mentioned in the previous paragraph, loving deliberately can embrace passion and agitation. In fact, I believe that even anger can play a huge part in loving deliberately. Anger, like stress and inflammation is necessary and even helpful at times, but if it is allowed to linger it can be deadly – just as stress and inflammation can be. This is especially true when the subject of one's deliberate love is a human animal. (By the way, I am not sure that losing one's temper with a non-human animal ever has any justification. I am confident that becoming angry with non-human beings can *never* lead to anything positive!) That said, perhaps some sustained forms of anger – if managed in an intentional, focussed way – can be constructive. I'm thinking of anger at malevolent forms of behavior: greed, intentionally maintained ignorance, bigotry, selfishness, cruelty. Doing so, I believe, can give real meaning to our appreciation of the very best qualities of human experience: generosity, the growth of knowledge, acceptance, tolerance, kindness. And this can, in turn, give our deliberate love – whether for a concept or practice (education, fighting ignorance or poverty, protecting the environment, for example) or a living being – so much more substance.

All of this probably sounds like it may be rather idealized. As a matter of fact, for me, it *is*. Loving deliberately is something I aspire to develop, something that can be nurtured and grown, but perhaps never truly perfected – almost like Enlightenment is to some spiritual beliefs/philosophies. As I embrace it and learn from it, I am becoming better at it. But I cannot say that the requisite patience and focus and purpose and consistency all come easily for me. Even when it comes to some of the people and things I love the most and, consequently, want most to love deliberately, I occasionally fall short. And that's OK. That all-important Self-love I spoke of earlier keeps me going and prevents me from being too hard on myself when I slip. Aspiring to be a deliberate lover, then, is akin to aspiring to be a Good Buddhist or a Good environmentalist or a Good parent or whatever path toward Goodness one may choose to follow. The key here, for me at least, is to be totally honest with and about my feelings and my efforts.

And now two final introductory thoughts. First, this one about the folks who have contributed to this project by sharing their thoughts and feelings in writing. I will confess that I came very close to making the decision to use recorded contributions in addition to written ones. But something that I cannot quite comprehend or explain kept me from doing so. That said, virtually every fellow traveller in the journey that has become this anthology has commented on the difficulty of the task. In fact, as you now know, some simply had to let it go … just too challenging; they simply could not find the words.[*] You see, my request to the contributors required introspection, probing, pain in some cases, a willingness to share, to put it

---

[*] To underscore this point, I want to share with you the words of a friend and a person I know to care a great deal about the subject of loving deliberately:

> Steven. Bob and I have been discussing your project for two sessions now and the task of defining loving deliberately is so vast and to me indescribable that I do not know what to say about it....no words.

Suzanne B.

all out there. Choosing to put pen to paper and to relate their responses via the written word – rather than talking to me and having me record their contributions – certainly added a huge challenge to providing their input. That said, it is comforting to me that virtually every person who tried to respond but had to let the task go was deeply grateful for the opportunity to take the task to heart, to think long and with great intensity about the subject, and to grow as a result.

As I have mentioned previously, one of the major differences between Studs Terkel's *Working* and our *Loving Deliberately* is the fact that all of the contributions within these pages were the product of the incredibly difficult act of *writing*. (Perhaps this act of writing about loving deliberately is also a manifestation of loving deliberately – in and of itself.) Providing *written* responses ups the ante dramatically. Some folks – even those whom I know to be exceptional writers – chose to *talk* to me about the topic. And those conversations, by mutual agreement, will remain our personal conversations ... not to be shared. Their responses are, of course, equally important and greatly appreciated and, yes, a vital part of this project even though they are not to be found explicitly within these pages. Moreover, I offer my most sincere gratitude to everyone who made the effort to contribute to this book – no matter what the final result of their efforts turned out to be.

And now my second parting thought – actually, more of an admission before we get into the heart of loving deliberately – about the contributions of those whose words you will read in the pages that follow. As I stated in the Preface, sometime after I made the decision to include only written contributions, I made another important decision: I decided to include the work of others who did not actually give me their permission to have their work included in this anthology.

Now, before I risk losing some of you owing to my admission of a seemingly shameful act of stealing the work of others who did not expressly consent to having their words appear in this anthology, here is the rest of the story. I have included the work of about twenty writers – some very well-known and some not – who either intentionally wrote for a large audience or intentionally wrote for a very intimate audience of one but whose work has become well read by many over time. At this writing, only one of the folks in this group is still with us. He is Lawrence Ferlinghetti whose masterful work "I Am Waiting" was impossible for me to leave out and whose permission – through his publisher – I actually *did* need to receive in order to include his poem. This was one of the last things that I did before completing the finishing touches for the publication of *Loving Deliberately*. I am hopeful that his words and those of all of the other contributors to this project prove to be a source of inspiration and reflection, if not sheer joy, for those of you who have chosen to spend some time with this book.

Part I

*Defining Loving
Deliberately ... Deliberately*

As you will see as you read on, I start each part of this anthology with a thought or two. Here I just want to comment on the positioning and length of the first part of this book for what should be obvious reasons. Specifically, I thought a good way to start would be to offer the work of some folks who chose to take on the task of defining what loving deliberately means, what it actually *is* – at least to them. This section has the largest number of offerings – by far – which probably makes sense considering the nature of the task at hand.

Loving Deliberately

Love is a seed planted, ready to sprout and grow. Deliberately cultivated and nourished, love grows and continues to persevere even in the midst of a storm. Love is resilient, its foundations unshaken by adversity. Love is decisive, continuously seeking the fertile truth, as falsehoods only twist and choke out its potency. Love is deliberate, demonstrating its unmatched power and strength as its roots grow deeply.

Loving deliberately gives us the opportunity to sow seeds in fertile ground every day of our lives. Loving deliberately is to feel love in everything we do, whether it is planting a garden, singing a song, talking with a stranger, or praying for an enemy. Loving deliberately is to accept that we all make mistakes, while acknowledging that we each must bear our own consequences.

Loving deliberately frees us to sow into all whose lives we touch with abundant joy. We make deliberate and careful choices to not only sow seeds of love, but to water, nurture and cultivate *that* which exemplifies the meaning our lives hold.

Love's harvest of faith, strength, healing, forgiveness, and mercy is only grown when we wisely care and tend to our gardens. Loving deliberately is to understand that left to itself, anything, including love, can begin to manifest and camouflage itself to be what it is not. Loving deliberately is to be watchful of that which seeks to destroy love, rather than to nourish it and watch it flourish. Loving deliberately is knowing how to love that which is unlovable.

Love is perfection. It sees beyond flaws. Love is faith. It can move mountains. Love is everlasting. It cannot be killed.

Without love, we merely exist. We are no different than the outer shell of an empty seed. Without the seed itself, nothing will grow from the shell. We cannot grow without love. Love is the seed of life and what gives up the opportunity to live an abundant life by loving deliberately.

God is love.

Selene Anderson
November 15, 2017

1. Be flexible, even when you know it's not in your DNA. Just thinking you are being flexible is probably an improvement on thinking you can't be.

2. Say you're sorry when you fuck up and MEAN it.

3. Listen more even if you were born with ONE ear and TWO mouths.

4. If you are lucky enough to have someone who really cares about you then you'd better work at maintaining that relationship. If you THINK you are working at it then you had better check that the other person thinks so too. I could be better at this.

5. If you are lucky enough to have kids then their welfare is actually MORE important than yours OR your partner's. Realising that has actually SAVED lots of marriages / relationships.

6. Loving a dog and looking after it is good practice for human relationships. Cats, meh, not so much……what were you THINKING???

7. I was going to write you a song but you didn't give me that option AND not enough words rhyme with DELIBERATELY! Of course, if I went down that track it was bound to be humorous and sarcastic and that just wouldn't do. Having said that…….I have 29 days left!

Mike Roberts
Eudunda, South Australia

Ode on a Grecian Urn

Thou still unravish'd bride of quietness,
    Thou foster-child of silence and slow time,
Sylvan historian, who canst thus express
    A flowery tale more sweetly than our rhyme:
What leaf-fring'd legend haunts about thy shape
    Of deities or mortals, or of both,
        In Tempe or the dales of Arcady?
    What men or gods are these? What maidens loth?
What mad pursuit? What struggle to escape?
        What pipes and timbrels? What wild ecstasy?

Heard melodies are sweet, but those unheard
    Are sweeter; therefore, ye soft pipes, play on;
Not to the sensual ear, but, more endear'd,
    Pipe to the spirit ditties of no tone:
Fair youth, beneath the trees, thou canst not leave
    Thy song, nor ever can those trees be bare;
        Bold Lover, never, never canst thou kiss,
Though winning near the goal yet, do not grieve;
    She cannot fade, though thou hast not thy bliss,
        For ever wilt thou love, and she be fair!

Ah, happy, happy boughs! that cannot shed
    Your leaves, nor ever bid the Spring adieu;
And, happy melodist, unwearied,
    For ever piping songs for ever new;
More happy love! more happy, happy love!
    For ever warm and still to be enjoy'd,
        For ever panting, and for ever young;
All breathing human passion far above,

That leaves a heart high-sorrowful and cloy'd,
    A burning forehead, and a parching tongue.

Who are these coming to the sacrifice?
    To what green altar, O mysterious priest,
Lead'st thou that heifer lowing at the skies,
    And all her silken flanks with garlands drest?
What little town by river or sea shore,
    Or mountain-built with peaceful citadel,
        Is emptied of this folk, this pious morn?
And, little town, thy streets for evermore
    Will silent be; and not a soul to tell
        Why thou art desolate, can e'er return.

O Attic shape! Fair attitude! with brede
    Of marble men and maidens overwrought,
With forest branches and the trodden weed;
    Thou, silent form, dost tease us out of thought
As doth eternity: Cold Pastoral!
    When old age shall this generation waste,
        Thou shalt remain, in midst of other woe
Than ours, a friend to man, to whom thou say'st,
    "Beauty is truth, truth beauty,—that is all
        Ye know on earth, and all ye need to know."

John Keats

Loving Deliberately

I love dark chocolate – I don't love it deliberately. I love your new outfit – I don't love it deliberately. I love some relatives and friends, and I don't necessarily love all of them deliberately either. I do love *myself* deliberately, and that means taking care of my body, mind, heart and soul – hard work every day.

Here are a few examples of loving deliberately that I have known:

- assuring your orphaned granddaughter with abandonment issues again that yes, you love her, even though she asks to the point of irritation

- and when that beloved grandmother is near the end, telling the doctors to treat her pain and let her go

- calling, emailing, and pouring out your thoughts in 7-page letters to your girlfriend as you try to win her heart

- massaging medicine into her arthritic feet every night before bedtime

- attending your child's sporting and school events no matter how many hours you worked

- working amicably with your ex on all issues that deal with your children

- saying no, and not enabling your child

- teaching your child to take responsibility for words and actions, allowing him to fail and being there as he picks himself up again

- after she passes, putting together a tribute booklet of your mom's best recipes, family photos, and vignettes about meals and family events

- holding a loved one at a distance because her addiction has completely taken over, costing repeated heartbreak, disappointment, worry, time, money, happiness –yours and others' whom you love

- listening to that positive inner voice and tuning out that negative one

Few people in my life get my deliberate love. Loving deliberately means investing my time, my tools, my emotional energy, my decision-making processes, MYSELF in someone else. It means loving with sacrifice and passion, consideration and intention– nurturing and preserving a relationship with someone across time. Loving another deliberately is risky, for it brings great joy and sometimes pain. There is great joy when someone loves me back deliberately and we change and grow together. There can also be intense pain upon loss of that love, or in the letting go. Perhaps there would be less pain if the love hadn't had that aspect of deliberateness, but then it would not have held the joy.

Anonymous
2017

Loving Deliberately

To feel Love is the same as feeling completely satisfied for even a moment. Love equals the absolute contentment that you feel when your selfish needs are accomplished either emotionally, spiritually, intellectually, or physically.

I believe in love. It is a force that drives us all. Humans were blessed with free will; this Love is selfish. Love is weakness.

Love is compromise. Simply put Love starts as satisfaction resulting in happiness.

Anonymous Twenty-eight year-old male

To love a partner deliberately means to sometimes direct one's actions and words with purpose. Along with what comes spontaneously in a mature, loving relationship, like smiles, affection, and sharing, that bond requires more. For example, there is compromise in small and large decisions and acceptance of differing opinions; not always saying what one is thinking, especially in emotionally charged situations; not sweating the small stuff, like leaving the cap off the toothpaste; paying attention to each other's moods and needs and then responding – or just listening – appropriately. These and other deliberate choices help sustain a loving relationship across time.

A parent-child relationship needs additional and different deliberateness, since parents must be more than friends to their children, and even adult children do not necessarily balance a relationship. From the start, parents have a multi-faceted job to love deliberately. This includes, but is not limited to, teaching responsibility, disciplining appropriately, modeling kindness and compassion, and sometimes intervening to save a life headed down a wrong or even dangerous path. Though the parental responsibility level changes over time, choosing to bring a child into this world should include choosing to love deliberately for decades.

61-year-old Female from Michigan

Love takes work. Love is a choice.

Being in a committed relationship has many fun moments but over time, the elation of "being in love" dissipates. It's almost a shame that society focuses so much on the excitement of falling in love rather than the process. Focusing on the "big event" of a wedding and all the TV programs like "Say Yes To The Dress" and having weddings that now span multiple days and exotic and expensive "bachelorette/groomsmen" weekends. This seems to make life thereafter such a letdown. What's so important is lost during that euphoric stage. At the risk of sounding negative, love is about the day to day, not the magical celebration.

This leads to my few steps after 38 years of being in a single committed relationship:
1) Love involves forgiving every day; neither spouse is perfect.
2) Love involves taking care of yourself first; if you are not happy with yourself, physically and mentally, you cannot spread happiness to others.
3) Love involves giving one compliment to your spouse every day, however insignificant it might be; amazingly that sometimes prompts a compliment in return and the feeling that you still matter.
4) Loves involves saying "thank you" regularly…how powerful those simple words can be.
5) Love involves staying compassionate and providing support daily.
6) Love involves knowing when to talk and when to stay silent. While talking often would seem more ideal, once you really come to know another, you realize

silence can sometimes be more powerful than words could ever be.
7) Love involves giving a little and being compassionate even in areas that may not seem important to you.
8) Love involves reminding yourself, especially in the hard times, that life is not necessarily greener in some other relationship. This is often difficult especially since we live so much longer these days.

In the end, love is work, hard work, and the plan to love each other for better or worse or for richer or poorer, in sickness and in health, is a conscious and deliberate choice. The idea that love should be constant, effortless, and euphoric is why so many relationships fail. Real life in a relationship is about weathering storms together; how we decide to weather those storms is the measure of the love we share.

People are always changing, growing, evolving. Love is a constant discovery process of yourself and the other. But that process makes life so much fuller. And while neither party to a relationship is perfect, choosing love makes life more meaningful and wonderful.

An anonymous quote sums it up: "No one falls in love by choice, it is by chance. No one stays in love by chance, it is by work. And no one falls out of love by chance, it is by choice."

Lucie-Anne Dionne-Thomas
(Middletown, Rhode Island, August 2018)

Loving Deliberately. I looked *deliberate* up. It said: "Done consciously and intentionally and fully considered." Yes, that is exactly what I did. I married my soulmate, who one year before our wedding, was told he had multiple sclerosis. John told me he would totally understand if I walked away. I fully considered that option and then consciously made the decision to continue loving him whether he could walk or not. After about twelve years, he could not. At about our 16th year, he got MRSA in a small wound he had from the wheelchair rubbing on his hip. The MRSA travelled deep into his hip bone and he was in four hospitals for TEN MONTHS, enduring ten surgeries. While John was fighting for his life in the hospital, our 22 year old son passed away. John couldn't come to the funeral. I didn't want to live any longer, but I had a 16 year old daughter who just lost her brother and who needed me to be strong and sane.

Loving deliberately came into play once again. I wanted to give up, not get out of bed, feel sorry for myself, join my son. But, I loved my daughter and realized I needed to love who was here. It wasn't easy, grieving the loss of our son, driving back and forth three hours to visit my very ill husband, trying to keep the house going and faking to my daughter that everything was alright. Everything, though, was all wrong. I stopped loving God. I was angry at Him. How could He take this amazing young man from us? Why did He give even more for my husband to endure? Why was He punishing me? I deliberately chose NOT to go to church anymore. I just tried to make it through each day, breathing in and breathing out. I would grocery shop at 10 p.m. at night so I wouldn't see anyone I knew . I didn't want to pretend to be strong and positive and happy. My friends and family fed my daughter and I hot meals from Feb. 14 (the night TJ died) until spring break. I would get home from the hospital and someone would have cut my lawn. I started believing that there really were a lot of GOOD and caring people in this world and something amazing started happening.

The very last thing my son said to me the afternoon I dropped him off at the train station to go back to dental school was: "I'm so sorry, Mom, that I am so weak that my 55 year old Mom has to carry my bag in for me. Someday, Mom, I promise…I will take care of YOU." I could write a book about how he kept his promise. It was just from Heaven. Miracle after miracle was whacking me in the head, until one day, I stood at the cemetery on his grave and it all became crystal clear. I realized that TJ was keeping his promise. John got better. Jessie, our daughter, ended up with a master's in social work and does a truly amazing job making a difference with her 75 Hospice patients. She called me one day saying, "Mom! How in the world did I end up doing this?! I wanted to train dolphins since I've been FOUR!!!" I told her life got in the way. She knew at her young age only too well what a serious illness does to a family and what losing a loved one feels like. I wrote a book about our son's illness and was on several TV programs and made numerous speeches. Because of the publicity of our story, I stopped counting after over 30 parents, desperate for help, came to my kitchen table. All but one put their child in a residential eating disorder center and helped to save a precious life.

I went back to church and I love God more than I ever did. I have a personal relationship with Him and my faith is deeper than I ever thought possible, once I let go of my anger and self-pity. I realize that we do not understand everything while on this Earth, but I do understand much more than I did before I had so many crosses to bear. So many times, it's

Defining Loving Deliberately … Deliberately

the people who have lost someone who develop a deep passion to reach out and help others. It's the people whose community has been destroyed by a tornado who all come together to help one another and the "stuff" becomes just "stuff" if their loved ones or pets are okay. It's those hanging from a cliff who finally turn to God. So many of us only turn to Him when we NEED him. Maybe that's why bad things happen. I heard a pastor once say: If your baby has a 102 degree fever, you give them Tylenol. If they have a 104 degree fever, we rush them to the ER. If they have 106 degree fever, we fall on our knees pleading with God.

I deliberately chose to love a man who had MS. We have been happily married for 27 years. I deliberately chose to believe my son had a much higher cause in his 22 years and until I see him again, I want to make him proud of me. I deliberately chose to keep on going for my incredible daughter, who now, I understand, stayed strong for ME at her young age of 16. I deliberately chose to continue living and laughing and loving. People tell me constantly how much I inspire them, and that makes me happy. I deliberately chose to lean on my faith for strength, and I feel so blessed.

Susan Barry

I learned to love from my grandmother, who invited me to her calmness, her peaceful generous view of the world beginning, as I recall, when I was four years old. She never had an unkind word to me, nor about anyone else. I recall the experience of being without worry and without having to wonder if I was OK.... as a child, finding out everything could be OK was new to me. As I reflect, I recognize the love was unconditional, with neither adrenaline nor drama, a peaceful experience.

My grandmother's undivided attention was captivating, I was so drawn, as a middle child of seven, undivided anything was impossible in our family. Whenever I returned home from college, or later with my children, I visited her first. She helped me slow down, my first experience of being in the moment. I was living in fast forward world, filling my moments with doing, not being.

I recognize now, that when I chose to change my career, to "give birth to my second half of life" I was intentionally choosing to practice the same, to offer my undivided attention to clients in therapy, to be in the moment.

Through my work with women caught up with domestic violence, I have witnessed thousands of women become aware, gradually, that they did not love themselves. As each person experienced a safe place to explore her past willingness to put herself last, I witnessed movement toward self love. Women considered the Five Love languages: words, gifts, touch, undivided attention and help. They were able to identify what their primary choice was to receive love and express love. They made more movement toward rejecting "power and control" as bankrupted love experiences. When asked if that kind of "love" would be OK for their sister, or mother, or best friend, there was a resounding "no" that confronted their own past willingness. The extraordinary transformation that occurred can be summed up, simply, as their beginning to love themselves. They each began to deliberately reject what had been passed off as love.

It is only now, through this reflection on deliberate love, I recognize that I intentionally chose to activate my Gramma Susie's love language in my life. Through my practice, there has been a shift for me from human doing to human being. I have a long way to go to be in the moment in my relationships, but I am better. I am deliberately choosing to be loving. That is step two for me.

Carol Wruble
December 2018

"Loving deliberately" might be something of an oxymoron – if not a paradox. If "loving" is an emotion, it cannot be enacted deliberately – only felt as natural and pure; it cannot be prescribed, controlled, parsed as if a grammar of incremental experience. However, the ***behavior*** of "loving" ***can*** be enacted deliberately – but then doesn't it cease to be "loving"? becoming instead something deliberate or intentional, such as caring, devotion, commitment?

> Stan Malless & Jane Kretko,
> professors emeriti,
> Simpson College
> Indianola, IA

June 10, 2018
Get nowhere fast. Get somewhere slow.

A relationship is an ever-changing unique experience and undeniable energy created by two people who follow rules of deliberation. You must nourish and care for all relationships or they will wilt and die.

Relationships are manifested through time and interactions, but not all relationships are created equally.

Have you ever felt that once in a lifetime tingle of meeting your true other? You'll freeze and dissociate from everything around you as your eyes tunnel vision. It's crazy and unreal, almost like every cell of your being is shouting, "I want to know everything there is to know about this person!!"

What does this feeling mean? That's what you now would like to find out.

Simply put, you want to try and they want to try with you.

That's where it starts and this also happens to be the easiest part.

Where it ends will be up to you two!

With every effortless and effort-filled interaction this relationship will grow and reach new levels.

Each level may or may not include acceptance, surprises, confessions, understanding, collaborating, letting go, attachment. Every corner you two will be faced with a choice... Is the juice worth the squeeze?

If it is, you will find beautiful solace in knowing the union you have with your other is built on mutual labor and a gradual incline of peeling back the layers of who you present yourself to be, to reveal who you truly are. Your authentic selves working to be happy and make each other happy in this exclusive and ever-changing love. Letting go of the bullshit and accepting life as a weird ride to manipulate into whatever you are building towards. Loving each other deliberately to accomplish happiness within each other and within your individual lives. Deliberate loving.

Kelsie Tamblyn
21
Brooklyn, NY

"When asked how they managed to stay together for over 50 years, the couple responded with 'we came from a generation where if something was broke, you fixed it, rather than exchanging it for the new model.'"

"When asked how she knew he was the one, she said 'Love isn't an emotion. Love is a verb. An action. Something that I choose every single day. You think I want to love this idiot when he forgot to get the milk we needed, or when he spent too much time at the arcade? Nah. But I do. I do because I've chosen to love him every day for nearly 2,000 days now, and I'm not stopping now. Not when he makes every morning brighter, every night warmer, and the scary things in life a little bit sillier.'"

"When asked about the bond he shared with his lifelong friend, he said 'I adopted him when he was just a pup. I went in to the shelter, and there was just something about his eyes. It was like he looked all the way into me: he saw the man I once was, the man I am, and the man I'm trying to be. I took him home because that didn't scare him. He was willing to support me and see my progress through. I look into his eyes now and I can see the support, the wisdom, but above all, his unconditional love for myself and the people he meets on our walks.'"

Marlo Scholten
October 2018

Loving deliberately (second attempt)

Well, let's give this another shot... switching over. I have used the word love a lot it my life; I love this or love that, I would love to do this or that... or I would love to do something or the other.

I think it takes a long time to figure out exactly what that seemingly simple word means, because we often don't really pause to define it. I think most of us rush life; involved in the minutia of daily existence we run from one existence to another. I would suggest that it is possible that some people never do get the chance to relate to something deliberate.

The word deliberate to me suggests with purpose and with care. So to Love deliberately would be to live one's life relishing in the process of existence. A full awareness and enjoyment of the treasure of awareness.

I don't believe that there is a correct way to love deliberately, but, whether it is a person, or hobby, or activity, it is to me valuing the action, process and result. I have been aware lately that some of the things I love to do, may have limits to how long I can continue to participate. This awareness makes the activity much sweeter and I am very aware of details I will build into memories... But, even this I am aware could be taken, so the process must also be savored and cherished immediately as well.

Since our time here is brief, our passions; of which I feel Love may be the highest achieved, must be treasured. There may have been a previous existence, or there may be a continued existence. But it is the here and now to be immersed.

One last afterthought about Loving deliberately, Relationships, particularly toxic ones... As a younger person, I held on to these... assuming that to give them up not only showed weakness on my part but also an unwillingness to hurt someone's feelings. Not that I am interested in hurting someone's feelings... but a toxic relationship can cause harm to both people. So, Loving sometimes means the deliberate acceptances of yourself, the need to let go of something no longer needed or serving a purpose. Yes, breaking the relationship. To me it is not shrinking away quietly, but explaining to the person, and then walking away. It is not important that they accept your decision as much as it is to move on and clear your life. This is often easier to understand in cleaning a closet, but it is the same principle.

Craig Weis

Everything is a choice.
We choose to get up in the morning.
We choose to go to work.
We choose to eat food and drink water.
You choose to read,
something that I chose to write,
that Steve Bannow chose to include in his wonderful book.

However, *love* is not a choice,
Unless your heart,
And mind,
Are one.

Back when I was in elementary school I always sat with my older brother on the bus ride to school. However he is 2 years older than me so I had to sit by myself for the other 2 years of elementary school. Normally I'd sit alone in the front of the bus and just talk and hang out with the bus driver until I noticed that someone else was doing the same. It was a little boy named James that was also in my class at the time. I would kinda watch him at first and wave every now and again until eventually we started sitting next to each other. We talked and played and talked some more about all sorts of things and one day I felt something. It was new and different. Warm. That was the first time that I experienced a crush. They say that your first crush is the biggest, and that they take up most of your heart. I guess my heart didn't listen very well because he had stolen it from me completely.

A word of advice:
Never tell your father about who you like.
Fathers can't keep secrets when it comes to these things.

James and I somehow got to the topic of love one day on our way home from school. He asked me, a 9 year old girl, what *love* is. I tried to give him the best answer I could but it took me nearly the whole ride to even form any sort of an answer. I was stumped. Love is taken too lightly in words, too deeply in feelings, and too complicated in thoughts yet simple in action. Then there is the end.

There was a girl named Shelby. She was the popular type. Sat in the back, 'pretty', very bossy, self-centered and everyone did what she wanted which apparently includes treating the boys around her like slaves or her own butlers. It might have been a game or it might not but "if *that* is what popularity looks like then I want no part of it." Is what I thought to myself. I'm not the type to bully or be mean so I just stayed quiet unless there is an injustice. The guys seemed to enjoy it so I said nothing. I guess someone else liked the popular type too. We never sat together after that. I thought it was the end and that was it. My deliberate love was over. Little did I know that my *love* for him wasn't actually over, it just wasn't deliberate anymore. My heart seemed like it flew off and stuck to his side, even now.

Time goes by and somehow I ended up making friends with his family, mother, brother, and father, but I still couldn't quite talk to him like we used to. His mom actually encouraged my love and said that she'll point out my house to James while going to and from church. I laughed just thinking about her actually doing that. Things kinda got better after that, he came over during lunch one time to kinda say hi and ask about church choir and wondered why I stopped but the conversation still felt stiff. By now he should have some idea of how I feel about him right? That was something I always thought about. *Was I too inconsiderate? Was I a burden? I wonder how he really feels about me. I feel like I should apologize for not talking to him more.*

Then it happens. We get a class together. It was a special ed. class, we go, work on homework, and study. There was a 13 colonies / the first 13 states test. The students were given a blank map and the name of the states on the side of the paper and you had to write them in the correct state. This was an 8th grade test that everyone in the history classes had to take. James and I were in history and the teacher that was in charge of our special ed class suggested that we sit down together at this small round table and study for the test. Suddenly by the end of the study session we were talking like we talked everyday of our lives. I had so much fun and I remembered why I loved him back in elementary school. His cute smile, lovely laugh, soft eyes and great personality, and that captivating sent. I ***loved*** him deliberately again, if only for just a moment until he asked the one question that I didn't want to hear.

'Wanna be friends?'

It hit me. Hard. I had tried to fall in love with others, I tried to have crushes, I tried so hard to just have friends. I accepted the real meaning of 'friends' in my school, say hi to them in the halls, do group projects if they can't find someone else, and don't ever expect to see them out of school. Expect not to be invited to do things and expect no one when you invite them. I wanted a real 'friend' but I wanted to be more than friends with him. My love, still, is unwavering even today but this shook my mind. I was transferring to a middle college program after that last year was up. We wouldn't even be able to say hi in the halls much less see each other. I wanted to say

YES. Oh, god how I wanted to say YES… but I wanted to be *more than friends*.

"No"

It was the only thing I said. I could have explained why I could have not looked at him in silence. I could have not walked away. But I did.

I keep wondering if I hurt his feelings that day. I want to say "I'm sorry. I didn't mean it like that." Or something but I didn't.

My feelings for him seemed to dull a little in time until he started to appear again. In my dreams. The day I turned 18 I was camping with my family we were all sharing tents. That night I had a dream. The kind of dream where you know who was in it and how you felt about the dream but don't really remember anything about it. I was in tears. My family was freaking out but I just laughed. They were tears of joy. I don't know what was in the dream but I *wish* so much that I did. All I remember was that he was there, I could even smell just a little of his unforgettable scent, and that I was so happy and warm, like I got the best hug ever. Sometimes I love him deliberately just to get that feeling back or just after I wake up from other dreams with him in it.

I have loved everyone else like family; like a cousin, a sister, an aunt, a mother, even a grandmother. I even love my enemies to the point where they wanted to be 'friends' with me because I thought if everyone is loved by someone, can't someone love everyone?

But my heart, my *love* are still his.

I love everyone deliberately.
I *Love* James whether it is deliberate or not.
No matter if I choose to,
Or not.

Note to James: If you ever read this, please know I am sorry for rejecting your friendship and I'm sorry if I was ever a bother to you. Just to let you know, I love you but I need a heart back. Either yours, or mine. I will still love you no matter what happens, the only difference is if it is *love* or love. However it is deliberate either way.

Deliberately:
consciously and intentionally; on purpose.
in a careful and unhurried way.

Rose Marie
November 2018

Winnipeg May 2017

I'm not sure that I would be much good at trying to come up with a definition of loving deliberately, but I have examples. I will share one with you.

When I was a little boy about 5 or 6 I think, my Granny who didn't have much money took in other folks' dirty laundry and washed and ironed the clothes in order to save the money to buy me my first pair of hockey skates for Christmas. Here's the kicker. The card said "with love and a big hug from Santa." She loved the spirit of giving and me so much that she was more than happy to give the credit for my favourite gift to someone else. I didn't find out what really happened until about six months after Granny passed away.

I guess loving deliberately can be caring and giving completely and unselfishly. I try to do this as often as I can.

My friends call me Gus

Home Burial

He saw her from the bottom of the stairs
Before she saw him. She was starting down,
Looking back over her shoulder at some fear.
She took a doubtful step and then undid it
To raise herself and look again. He spoke
Advancing toward her: "What is it you see
From up there always—for I want to know."
She turned and sank upon her skirts at that,
And her face changed from terrified to dull.
He said to gain time: "What is it you see,"
Mounting until she cowered under him.
"I will find out now—you must tell me, dear."
She, in her place, refused him any help
With the least stiffening of her neck and silence.
She let him look, sure that he wouldn't see,
Blind creature; and awhile he didn't see.
But at last he murmured, "Oh," and again, "Oh."

"What is it—what?" she said.

"Just that I see."

"You don't," she challenged. "Tell me what it is."

"The wonder is I didn't see at once.
I never noticed it from here before.
I must be wonted to it—that's the reason.
The little graveyard where my people are!
So small the window frames the whole of it.
Not so much larger than a bedroom, is it?

There are three stones of slate and one of marble,
Broad-shouldered little slabs there in the sunlight
On the sidehill. We haven't to mind *those*.
But I understand: it is not the stones,
But the child's mound—"

      "Don't, don't, don't, don't," she cried.

She withdrew shrinking from beneath his arm
That rested on the banister, and slid downstairs;
And turned on him with such a daunting look,
He said twice over before he knew himself:
"Can't a man speak of his own child he's lost?"

"Not you! Oh, where's my hat? Oh, I don't need it!
I must get out of here. I must get air.
I don't know rightly whether any man can."

"Amy! Don't go to someone else this time.
Listen to me. I won't come down the stairs."
He sat and fixed his chin between his fists.
"There's something I should like to ask you, dear."

"You don't know how to ask it."

      "Help me, then."

Her fingers moved the latch for all reply.

"My words are nearly always an offense.
I don't know how to speak of anything
So as to please you. But I might be taught

I should suppose. I can't say I see how.
A man must partly give up being a man
With women-folk. We could have some arrangement
By which I'd bind myself to keep hands off
Anything special you're a-mind to name.
Though I don't like such things 'twixt those that love.
Two that don't love can't live together without them.
But two that do can't live together with them."
She moved the latch a little. "Don't—don't go.
Don't carry it to someone else this time.
Tell me about it if it's something human.
Let me into your grief. I'm not so much
Unlike other folks as your standing there
Apart would make me out. Give me my chance.
I do think, though, you overdo it a little.
What was it brought you up to think it the thing
To take your mother-loss of a first child
So inconsolably—in the face of love.
You'd think his memory might be satisfied—"

"There you go sneering now!"

"I'm not, I'm not!

You make me angry. I'll come down to you.
God, what a woman! And it's come to this,
A man can't speak of his own child that's dead."

"You can't because you don't know how to speak.
If you had any feelings, you that dug
With your own hand—how could you?—his little grave;
I saw you from that very window there,

Making the gravel leap and leap in air,
Leap up, like that, like that, and land so lightly
And roll back down the mound beside the hole.
I thought, Who is that man? I didn't know you.
And I crept down the stairs and up the stairs
To look again, and still your spade kept lifting.
Then you came in. I heard your rumbling voice
Out in the kitchen, and I don't know why,
But I went near to see with my own eyes.
You could sit there with the stains on your shoes
Of the fresh earth from your own baby's grave
And talk about your everyday concerns.
You had stood the spade up against the wall
Outside there in the entry, for I saw it."

"I shall laugh the worst laugh I ever laughed.
I'm cursed. God, if I don't believe I'm cursed."

"I can repeat the very words you were saying:
'Three foggy mornings and one rainy day
Will rot the best birch fence a man can build.'
Think of it, talk like that at such a time!
What had how long it takes a birch to rot
To do with what was in the darkened parlor?
You *couldn't* care! The nearest friends can go
With anyone to death, comes so far short
They might as well not try to go at all.
No, from the time when one is sick to death,
One is alone, and he dies more alone.
Friends make pretense of following to the grave,
But before one is in it, their minds are turned
And making the best of their way back to life

And living people, and things they understand.
But the world's evil. I won't have grief so
If I can change it. Oh, I won't, I won't!"

"There, you have said it all and you feel better.
You won't go now. You're crying. Close the door.
The heart's gone out of it: why keep it up.
Amy! There's someone coming down the road!"

"*You*—oh, you think the talk is all. I must go—
Somewhere out of this house. How can I make you—"

"If—you—do!" She was opening the door wider.
"Where do you mean to go? First tell me that.
I'll follow and bring you back by force. I *will!*—"

From *North of Boston* (1914)
By Robert Frost

September 2018

Most of us have read or heard warnings (for lack of a better term) about making sure that we *tell* people we love that we love them every time we part company for our work day or when someone goes off on a trip or even a drive to the store. The lesson in all of this is that it just may be the last time that we see each other alive, and there will be no more chances to *tell* the other person how we feel. Most of us will also agree that such parting comments for those who practice this often ritualistic manner of parting usually say something uninspiring and routine like "Love ya." By doing so, they are off the hook, covered with no guilt about not professing their love during the potentially final encounter. Are these folks loving *deliberately?* At the risk of sounding callous, I will say that, if this is a key component in their practice of loving deliberately, they are missing the point. If we deliberately *demonstrate* our love consistently and often by touching with compassion, speaking meaningfully, taking an active interest, listening carefully, being unselfish, using the words "I love you" in a truly meaningful and *deliberate way,* then we are loving deliberately ... and catch phrases like "Love ya" are unimportant irrelevancies. It's all about the intentional *doing* loving.

Chris C.
Columbia, South Carolina

Loving deliberately? I find it difficult to empathise with the idea.

After 49 years of marriage I am not quite sure where to begin and what it all means. What is love? What makes it last and what causes it to fail? Rarely if ever have we (my wife is Sue) discussed the subject. And never have we put pen to paper on this subject. Somewhat an expert in creating military appreciations, business plans and financial spreadsheets, I have never wanted to or needed to examine this subject.

As a young man I entered the military academy in Australia and became an Infantry officer, Lieutenant, at the age of 19, just as Australia was increasing her commitment to the war in South Vietnam. I was young, immature, impetuous and foolish. I was pretty normal amongst my peers. Life was fast and the 60s was the decade of free love - or so we were told but did not really experience so freely.

I was chasing anything in a skirt. Almost every girl looked good to me. It was just pure lust. There was no consideration of future or long term or marriage or commitment. Sue looked good to me and she was a fun person to 'go out with'. She was learning modern dance as a hobby with the Sydney Arts Council and she was a secretary at the University of Sydney - where all the free love was supposed to be happening.

We started going out together on my return from Vietnam. Initially I don't think I was her only boy friend but we had lots of fun at pubs and night clubs and she visited my officers' mess for typically drunken parties and balls, so our relationship developed - always at a very relaxed and casual level. For heavens sake, I was not 21 years old and was just back from Vietnam.

Think we underestimate the amount of serendipity that influences our lives and if I hadn't been bored with my battalion life in Australia and hadn't impetuously marched myself into the Admin major's office and asked for a posting to Papua New Guinea (PNG) it is hard to know where I would be now. Indeed, impetuosity has been a significant trait, not always with positive outcomes. An hour later had my orders-join 2nd Battalion The Pacific Islands Regiment in Wewak, PNG in three months time.

Anyway, I called Sue (from my battalion post 140 miles away) and said "I'm going to New Guinea, would you like to come". She immediately replied "I'll be in that …."

Sue hung up and burst into tears. Her mother asked her what was wrong and she replied "Stewart is going to PNG and he wants me to go with him". "What does he mean" she asked. "He wants to marry me". Shocked, her mother said "I'll have to get to like the boy". At that stage we had only been courting for six months.

So that was that. No appreciation of the situation. No thoughts about the complex series of considerations and responsibilities. No thoughts of the longterm. We didn't even consider the impact on our parents caused by going to PNG for probably three years. Sue's Dad had died four months before.

To cut a long story short, my 21st birthday party became an engagement party (to my father's great surprise). Sue borrowed a dress and an old Rolls Royce car. Friends were invited to be brides maids and grooms and we were married in a church a month later. The fact that most of the guests suffered food poisoning at the catered wedding breakfast at Sue's Mum's home was nothing to worry about (I didn't eat anything so I was ok). I spent the money from selling my car on a skiing honeymoon and I was soon off to Papua New Guinea.

I have to say there was a bit of emotion in the lead up to the wedding - girls are like that- and after the wedding as we tried to adjust to married life with me 140 miles away at my post and preparing to leave the Country. Sue had never lived away from home, done any serious housework or had to Cook for herself on a continuous basis.

Stewart Penny
Buderim, QLD

Loving deliberately …. what?!?!? Maybe had I actually loved deliberately, I might not have been married three times. No, I love with my whole heart, unconditionally, and without seeing the whole picture. I am trusting, or used to be. I am giving, or used to be. I am accepting, or used to be. I only see the best in people, or used to.

The love of my life moved away before I graduated from college. He asked me to marry him but I had one more year of college left. At the time, that was not acceptable in my family and group of peers. I thought he would stay and wait one more year, but he really DID make the move. Strike one.

Strike two. My father died two years prior and my mother was very needy. Before my dad died, he asked me to take care of my mom. I loved my dad more than I ever thought possible. His death left a huge void in my life. He was my rock.

Strike three. My boyfriend was too far away, we did not have cell phones in those days, and Skype was not an option. Whoever said, "Distance makes the heart grow fonder", had not a clue!

After college graduation. I moved to the Detroit area for my first teaching position to prove to my mother I was worthy of my parents' college investment. My boyfriend was starting his second year in Florida. He was a lifeguard at Daytona Beach and a substitute teacher waiting for a teaching position to open. Time was not on our side. He was lonely and started dating a girl he worked with at the beach. Then, he moved in with her. Wow! Back in those days, girls who moved in with guys had only one name. So sad how our family morals had so much affect on our lives. I was, needless to say, heart broken.

We remained friends for forty years. He would always stop to see my mom when he was in town visiting his parents. From time to time, I would receive a call to say he never stopped loving me. I was usually married … to someone else. hahaha He was married with children, so I knew our friendship could go nowhere but a friendly call. We kept up with each others job accomplishments, family births, deaths, and inner most thoughts and concerns.

2008, I was exhausted. I had been assigned all the middle school music classes and choirs, and all the high school choral groups. My mother had a heart attack and could not stay alone at night. So, I stayed at my mother's every night never getting any sleep. My husband's indiscretions had once again come to the forefront. This had gone on for sixteen years. My precious son was completely unhinged by this situation, as was his mother. My health was not good but could never find the cause. My best friends had an actual "intervention" for me. They said I had to learn how to say "NO" and cut back on my commitments. Well, my friends saved my life. I decided to take early retirement and move out of town. I wanted to move to Florida in 1974, so finally decided to do so.

2009, I was Florida bound. But, I was still exhausted all the time. While seeing a dermatologist in Florida for an unrelated problem, he noticed a spot on my leg. Said he thought it was melanoma and did a biopsy right then and there. Diagnosis came back Melanoma Stage IIIB. After surgery and chemotherapy, another spot appeared. Then, cancer was discovered in my lymph nodes. Now, it was Melanoma Stage IV. The reason for my exhaustion was now apparent. "Everything happens for reason" is absolutely true! I was treated, as a last option, with two hyperthermic limb perfusions. This treatment was only done in three places in the US. Tampa being one of those three. My life was spared. The love of my life found me and moved in to take care of me. It was a miracle any of this happened. We are together after forty years of friendship. Life is good. I am loving deliberately.

Anonymous

The Deliberateness of Loving

Loving deliberately comes from a great depth of compassionate experience and exchange of all those with whom one encounters on the path within one's life. And, as well, all throughout their existences in this journey embarked upon from the moment of first breath until at last there is breath no more. In the beginning, helpless babes do all the receiving of deliberate love, thus preparing, instilling, training, and equipping the innocent soul to ultimately return that love, as is the nature of growth in love is inevitable. Thus, each exchange of pouring love into the baby will guarantee an eventual outcome of love's pure intention from the baby's caretaker. As a baby grows into a child, each human meeting provides yet still another opportunity for the child to learn how to love intentionally, even though the child is unaware of such goings on. Then, there are times when the child understands exactly what the gift of love is all about. For example, as in the following case of Rose, if Rose's parent defends her when she had an unfortunate incident with a first-grade teacher, grabbing Rose by the arm which in turn inflicted nail gouges and the mother confronted the guilty teacher on the issue, though the mother did little most of the time on Rose's behalf, this defense would stand out to the six year old for the rest of her life. This was an example of defensible and deliberate love.

As the third and last child growing up in the 50s and 60s, Rose's mother of the household was no longer interested in being a mother and was frequently absent from the daily grind of this traditional societal occupation. So then, what does the absence of nurturer teach a child about deliberate love? Personally, with each moment of presence the child had with her, was an amazingly treasured gift. A child this age can only think the best and purest thoughts of her mother, no matter what bad choices that mother had made. This case was no exception, for most every child feels exactly the same way when it comes to their mother. Credit is due, of course, to the preparation of that love from the father. A father's love and respect for his wife and mother of his children make all the difference in the world to the individual child. For without it, the compass of love born in the child's heart is off-centered.

Hope is also instilled into the child by either one or both parents. Taking into consideration in the singular case of Rose, the child being discussed, and in this child's particularly unique situation, the mother would leave the home every evening dressed like a movie star, the child would then look out the window and watch, as her mother drove away. "Where is Mommy going?" "She'll be back" was the answer from her daddy. Hope believes the outcome will turn out all right in the end, especially in the young child's mind. Later, growing into the teen years, the child, having been trained by her father to love her mother unconditionally and deliberately, due to her father's example, confronted her mother but the incident was totally denied by her mother anything was wrong. One thing led to another, and with this rejection, Rose the teenager ran away. She was eventually caught and ultimately put into a boarding school by the guilt-ridden mother. Months passed, and the teenager was returned home. Still, the mother was in denial and kept up her wrong doing to the point of total humiliation by bringing a boyfriend into the home and in the presence of her husband. Deliberate love demands forgiveness.

Only, the teenager could not comprehend such love. Rebellion set in and the teenager became pregnant at 16 years old. Now, the guilt of the mother had been transferred onto the daughter for an outlet of the whole family. The teenager became a mother of three by age of 21. By this time, forgiveness set in towards her mother, and the daughter with a family of her own, now had the frightening experience of her baby nearly dying. As the daughter cried out to the God of the universe to save her 11-month-old son from dying, God whose deliberate love extended even to this rebellious daughter, answered her prayer, re-instated her baby's health, and saved the daughter's eternal soul through the experience. Thus, the daughter began to be equipped to carry on the value of the heavenly father's deliberate love because of Jesus' sacrifice on the cross to pay for the sins of the world and through his deliberate love saved this rebellious daughter for her in turn, to live out a life of deliberate love.

This new-found deliberate love began to be cultivated in the daughter's own little family's life. It has been said teen marriages do not last. Sadly, the embracement of faith was only on the young mother's part, and instead of receiving deliberate love, the mother and her three children were left destitute. However, the church where the mother had begun to attend gave the mother new-found hope through *their* deliberate love. By helping her to find a home for herself and her children, the purchase of a car and an established factory job, the woman was finally able to grow as a human being and continue to share deliberate love with those new acquaintances who she encountered daily. There is always a choice when expressing deliberate love: either it can be shared with all those with whom life's path has crossed, or the love can be diminished by the bitterness of what one's life path has been dealt.

Being a single mother of three, working in a factory, attending church weekly, and raising those three children had its challenges, but deliberate love conquers all and soon new acquaintances came into her life and one even proposed marriage. Theirs was a mutual vision to which both agreed in taking Bibles to then Communist Russia. Both marriage and the Russian trip were accomplished. And within six months after a fourth child was born, the woman found herself entering the border of Russia, where the Russian guards found 50 Russian new testaments hidden in her suitcase. Caught at the border with smuggled Bibles back then (1980) was forbidden and considered a felony in the USSR! Many years later, she still wonders why she was not taken to Siberia and forever lost in that frozen wasteland!

The release from detainment was to come later that day and an invitation to go to the Moscow Baptist State Church where the privilege to meet the vice-president of the Billy Graham's Association organization was extended. The man confirmed the Bibles would be sold in the underground for a month's wages to those Russians who greatly desired to have one. Consequently, back home to America, for the next 15 years, deliberate love did not exist in the young woman's experience. Instead, she had to learn how to prepare, instill, train, and equip her own soul to ultimately return deliberate love, though not reciprocated, as growth is inevitable in such unfortunate life circumstances which the woman found herself facing. Yet, deliberate love conquers all and for the next 16 years, the woman found how to love deliberately, even though in the end, it was no longer shared.

There she was, a woman left alone in an uncaring, cold, and indifferent world. And yet, deliberate love prepares, instills, trains, and equips such a woman so she can endure what life sends her way. Now that the other children were fully grown, to support herself and her last child, many jobs were taken but many more were lost, until one day at her then current position she met her future professor husband to be. As circumstances would have it, the woman was about to lose yet another job, when in he walked, and it was pure and deliberate love that found the woman. For it is true that what one sows, it shall be reaped, especially where deliberate love is at work.

After proposing marriage, the professor husband invited the woman to go to college. "Have you never been to college?" "Never." "Well, we'll have to remedy that!" And in January of the year 2000, the woman, for the first time in her life, crossed the hallowed halls of higher education. It was the beginning of a life-long journey which just recently was completed in the acquiring of a Ph.D. in higher education (August 10, 2018)! All the while, back in 2005, the earning of a master's degree in English Language and Literature, the woman was hired to teach English Composition. After 13 years, she is still impassioned with passing on the skill of writing to incoming students. The adventure of deliberate love has proven itself repeatedly in the woman's life and she is so happy to have learned to share, live and love unconditionally because there is really no other way than to live a life of deliberate love.

Anonymous 2019

Hello Steve, sorry this is behind schedule ....Paul has been in the hospital for the better part of a week....another by pass.... actually two. A new one just above his left knee ...about 10 inches or so of gortex and a replacement by pass further up... for one he had a few years ago. This helped the blood flow in his left leg tremendously! He has to be able to walk our youngest daughter down the isle in July..... His other leg could use the same surgery but I doubt if they will do another before July. I've been thinking a lot about what loving deliberately means to me. Perhaps Not loving deliberately is something to explore first. Such as ... Making a choice not to love Aunt Grace because she wasn't nice to me when I was growing up....or making a choice to be unfaithful to your spouse ...both deliberate actions not to love someone as they may want to be loved. When I met Paul... 50 some years ago... I knew I would love him forever... come hell or high water...that is loving deliberately... Going through life's ups & downs with a partner Time after time ......good times & bad...I knew I had made my choice the first time I saw him...to love deliberately.

I feel the same way about my friends & family.....I committed myself to loving them deliberately without hesitation when they came into my life as a small child...& the friends I've made as an adult ....they all have my love deliberately & unconditionally.

Further.....I believe that loving life deliberately brings peace to my life. I have surrounded myself unknowingly... With like-minded people.

I hope this makes sense Steve... Good luck with the book.....I'm already looking forward to loving it deliberately......cause you wrote it!!

Take care! Love Linda

This is for my Brother Steve's book.

For me, Loving Deliberately means caring for a being or a thing very deeply, with the strongest emotional feeling. It is more powerful than anger or hatred or any other feeling. This caring is constant because I choose it to be that way.

Here are the beings and things that I Love Deliberately. There is no order, just a very important list:

I love my family – deliberately.

I love my God – deliberately.

I love my close friends – deliberately.

I love my country – deliberately.

I love the forest – deliberately.

I love the mountain – deliberately.

I love the animals of Serengeti and Ngorongoro – deliberately.

I love my culture – deliberately.

I love my work – deliberately.

I love my self – deliberately.

From Aenea Makoninde (Tanzania)

Loving Deliberately Reflection
by Ashton-Ezra Stardust

If you had asked me before today what I think Loving Deliberately means then I wouldn't know how to fully answer myself. Now I think I have a better idea on what it truly means to love deliberately.

Deliberately implies a choice, doing something with a purpose to make it happen. Naturally that train of thought could be applied to the term Loving Deliberately. In that way, it would be like choosing to love but it feels like there is so much more to it than that.

Yesterday I met the love of my life in person for the first time in our almost five years of knowing each other. Not everyone believes a long-distance relationship can produce a real love. That the physical contact between two people is the key ingredient to create a lasting relationship and a lasting love, but they're wrong. Physical contact, while absolutely amazing, is more like a bonus that people take for granted. Love itself goes deeper than that, Loving Deliberately goes even deeper.

Loving Deliberately is making the conscious choice to choose love over all else. In keeping my long-distance relationship in mind, loving deliberately is choosing to love even when it gets hard. When the distance seems to great or we get in a fight because of one dumb thing or another; we still choose love. Honestly, it hasn't always worked out that way but even when we fall apart, we still find a way back to ourselves because we aren't willing to stop loving each other so easily.

I feel that love is the same way in all aspects of life. It isn't easy. Love is difficult and even more so to choose when there are easier options to go with instead. It's so much easier to choose hate rather than to love and accept someone who is different or who does wrong. It's easier to give up on a difficult relationship than to keep fighting to make it work. Even now, in today's society, it's almost easier to avoid love than to embrace it at all.

Loving Deliberately says no to all of that. It is possible to Love Deliberately and to do amazing at it. It's almost like a way of life that once it gets going, it's not impossible to keep it up. Why? Life is better with love. No matter how bitter a person, their fondest memories or fondest part of life usually revolves around a time when they were loved or had love.

Love makes us better people. Loving Deliberately is the conscious choice to do better and to live better in the name of love. And that's pretty amazing.

Gabe's Reflection:

Gabe thought of what to say next. "You need to start loving deliberately."

Damon straightened and did a double take at him. "You want me to do...what?"

"Love Deliberately," he repeated. How to explain it? Start with the basics. "Loving deliberately is more than just loving someone or being loved. It's so much more than that. Loving deliberately is looking at all the darkness and violence you could choose and going with love instead.

The world gives us so many reasons and excuses to avoid love; it tries to make it seem like love is only for a select few and impossible for others, but it's wrong. Loving deliberately is looking passed all the rhetoric and embracing love even when it's hard.

I'm not saying go out there and kiss every cute person you meet. I'm saying that you don't have to live with all this anger in your heart because life hasn't been kind to you. You can choose to do better. You can forgive the wrongs of life and start healing. You can let people in again and let them help you instead of pushing them away. You don't have to forgive everyone who you still hate, that will take time. A good first step is choosing to forgive yourself. You don't have to be your own worst enemy. You can choose to finally start working on loving yourself, because you are an amazing human being. You deserve to love yourself and see what everyone else who cares about you sees when they look at you.

Loving deliberately comes in different forms. You don't have to do them all, just start with one and I bet that life will start getting better faster than you think."

Damon ran a hand through dark locks before he responded. "That sounds hard to do."

Gabe just smiled and took his hand. "Good thing you're not doing it alone then."

Gabe's reflection/advice about Loving Deliberately without the story aspects:

"Love Deliberately," he repeated. How to explain it? Start with the basics. "Loving deliberately is more than just loving someone or being loved. It's so much more than that. Loving deliberately is looking at all the darkness and violence you could choose and going with love instead."

The world gives us so many reasons and excuses to avoid love; it tries to make it seem like love is only for a select few and impossible for others, but it's wrong. Loving deliberately is looking passed all the rhetoric and embracing love even when it's hard.

I'm not saying go out there and kiss every cute person

you meet. I'm saying that you don't have to live with all this anger in your heart because life hasn't been kind to you. You can choose to do better. You can forgive the wrongs of life and start healing. You can let people in again and let them help you instead of pushing them away. You don't have to forgive everyone who you still hate, that will take time. A good first step is choosing to forgive yourself. You don't have to be your own worst enemy. You can choose to finally start working on loving yourself, because you are an amazing human being. You deserve to love yourself and see what everyone else who cares about you sees when they look at you.

Loving deliberately comes in different forms. You don't have to do them all, just start with one and I bet that life will start getting better faster than you think.

Damon's Reflection:

Loving Deliberately? How should I know? I guess it sounds like a strategy? Maybe it's a way to get through life. I've tried doing the opposite: living a life without love or the people who love me most. It sucked. Can I say that for this? Anyway, loving deliberately makes me think of my adoptive parents. They're the nicest and most loving people I know. They didn't have to take me in or care for me the way they did but they chose to anyway. They chose to love me. They choose love a lot now that I think about it. Maybe loving deliberately is living more like them, by putting people first and choosing to try and understand someone instead of being prejudiced. I still don't get what loving deliberately could really be, but I think if more people lived with a phrase like that in mind this world would be a lot less dark than it is.

I find that love can blur matters when I really truly love someone. My love for the person actually spurs me into action. When I think of loving deliberately I think about the decade my husband, Andy, and I sacrificed our new marriage and other things like having children to take care of both of my incapacitated, elderly parents. My mom was 75 years old at the time and had Alzheimers. My dad was 82 years old and a stroke victim when they both came to live with us. We had only been married a year. I left my real estate career behind to care for my parents 24/7. None of us were prepared for the burdens and crisis that would lay ahead of us. The late-night emergency room visits, the doctor's appointments that took all day, the do-or-die surgeries, the endless urinary track infections that lead to delirium, the sudden falls with subsequent 911 calls, the endlessness of renewing prescriptions, keeping track of medical bills and the list goes on and on. Taking care of my parents until they each died with me by their side in 2009 (my father in February and my mother in December) was the biggest example of loving deliberately for me. Luckily, I married a kind, generous man that loved my parents deliberately as well, and contributed daily to their delicate care. In turn, my parents adored and loved him. Despite the scariness of some of the challenges we faced, I would do it again because that is what you do for someone you love...deliberately.

Amy

Loving deliberately

Loving deliberately is a path that many follow, but do not admit!

This is the "good" path, the path taken by very many throughout the world and as in many things it is its own reward. This is the good news; regrettably this does not sell newspapers, get shown on television, or brought up in conversation.

The easy path is to be negative, to not take that chance, to not, let others know who you really are, and not to honestly express yourself without purposely offending others. I was fortunate enough to be brought up in a household with strong work ethics and independence; told that quitting is permanent, if it is worth doing, give it everything you have.

I was never an outstanding book learner, I need to see and work with new knowledge, I am a doer. What I love is to learn! To educate myself, and enjoy the experience as I do. I have done this in various ways, at first by holding over twenty different jobs and small businesses, most at the same time. I also pursued learning formally, through college (BBA in Business) and tech school, (AD, RN nursing degree at 58 yrs. old). All the time while having a family in tow, great kids (two girls) and a loving wife. I failed (financially) more than succeeded; but gained wisdom through persistence and honesty. Nothing is easy that is really worth anything, and since learning is my passion, I try to experience as much as possible.

I was also lucky in early life to be my own person, to live the honest, giving, and positive life. To learn more, you have to give more, to love more you need to give more love, I keep telling my grandson that the "gift" is in the "giving", not the actual item. (At 11, He still is a little sceptive of this!)

Now that I am at an age of less flexibility (67); I have

turned to travel to further my love for education and traveling, throughout the United States (We have been to all 50) and the world (Over 40 countries and islands visited) I have learned that most people are "people". They want to be good, share, and take care of family and friends.......I guess this would be a natural love. Love is returned, give and you will receive, love is felt, being positive and trusting; far more rewarding than negative and overly cautious.

Married over forty-five years, after dating my wife for five years the secret to this loving deliberately is commitment and respect. She is she, don't try to change who she is, work with one another, support one another, no matter what, and be faithful, and thank one another regularly and often for who they are. We were born with two ears and one mouth, listen more and talk only when you have something to say, worth saying!

Grow together, talk to one another, and respect the others concerns and opinions.

Noah

Loving Deliberately

It is difficult for me to say what *loving deliberately* means to me without talking about what *love* is in my mind, and what *deliberate* might mean. I find it proper to address the whole without first investigating its parts.

Deliberate is an intentionality. It involves a sort of emotional and often physical labor and work. It is something that is not easy or necessarily natural. Though perhaps it is more natural and less quick; it is fair to reason that many natural processes occur slowly so I revise the former note. It implies that a length of time must be present, in which to do that work which is required to make a thing deliberate. Though I find that that work might often be unseen and may even be the work of patience and stillness. Yet, in other times deliberateness can manifest in times of great action.

Love is a much trickier term and I think I will take this entire (still too short) passage of text to attempt to capture its meaning. For the time we can adopt the dictionary's diagnosis of love which is an "intense feeling of deep affection".

As a Christian I hear the term *love deliberately* most weekends, it is often talked of in terms of *agape love* and is revered in my church as something beautiful and complicated and messy, that must be worked for and labored over; and, through that intent, by loving in a way that does not come easily, it is endowed with great spiritual worth.

As an asexual (and a romantic asexual at that) the idea of *love* itself can be very big and frightening, fairly uncomfortable, and more complicated than any physical basis. I have never known and have no desire to know *eros* nor *ludus* as the ancient Greeks called the deep passion of lovers and the frivolous games of lovers respectively. I have hardly even known *philia* which is a platonic love between friends. (When it comes to the Greeks I do not find that they have a proper word for *loving deliberately* but that all their forms of love may be done in a way that could be called deliberate.)

I find myself wondering, in the darker winters of my soul, if I can love at all. In many ways I find myself in the antithesis of *loving deliberately* as I try to avoid the feeling of romantic love, because I know it would be ultimately unfair to whomever I might feel affection for because I would ultimately deny him no matter how deeply I cared for him. No, there isn't any beautiful passion of love in my future. Even if I do (and I do) feel an emotional draw to romance that is based in the brain and heart. I am only hindered by this apathetic body that seems to trap my mind and soul.

Yet, in other ways, I find myself loving, perhaps, more deliberately than others simply because I must think of it, because it does not come naturally to me. I wonder "*Do I love; can I love? What if I were to have children, could I love them? Do I even love the family I have now?*" Still, I have always put the meager relationships I do possess above all else in my life. If I get the opportunity to spend a day with my mother I will put off work. The chance to spend an hour with my dad, I will endure the pains that come with that hour. To spend time with my brother, I will pass by many recreational plans before I turn him down. Is that not some semblance of love? Is it, if nothing else, at least intentional? And is intentionality not the highest necessity of love? But again you cannot force yourself into a feeling. But perhaps we have more control over emotions (those that a set deeper than the impulsive responses that are feelings) than feelings. Might it be possible to will myself into love?

Still I do not think these faults disqualify me from speaking on the subject. *Loving deliberately*, after all, does not require that type of love that occurs between lovers and even without the wisdom of experience I am a well-worn watcher of people and think I have gathered expertise in that way.

I believe deliberate love to be the love of time-tested love. No marriage lasts without love that is labored over. Love is not meant to come easily; there are the first months when things come simply and a rosy colors, but this is nothing more than simple pleasure, nearly leisure. It is what so many teenagers mistake for love and so they have many loves, and their heart continuously breaks superficially. (Now, let me add, that when I say 'superficially' I don't meant that the pain of such heartache is not severe and real, but only that it is not so deep nor so lasting as the heartbreak of deliberate love in which the broken one has done all that could be done to save his/her heart, but was left in spite of this, in total despair, in grief for the future that can no longer be. The loss of a love that was not labored for, leaves hardly a mark on the soul and might be washed away with simple tears and ice cream. The love of one who was fought for is a shellshock, when the soldier has returned from war on the losing side, having nothing to show for his/her sacrifices and bravery.

There is something in deliberate love that marks the soul, as if in our work we share pieces of one another with each other. Of course, I don't only speak of romance when I say this. Friendships also share a deeply deliberate love. (I might add that any love that persists over time is deliberate, and perhaps it is the very act of persisting together that fuses the bond between friends and partners.)

To love deliberately is to think of those around you, to want to improve and deepen your relationships, and to work toward doing that. I've heard friendships described before in terms of treble and bass. That most people whom you become aquatinted with interact with you in treble levels of existence. It is not something that is any less real or genuine but only something with less substance and depth. But then there are those people who you find you can turn up the bass with. These bass relationships, I find, are the more deliberate ones, in which the real vulnerable parts of yourself are borne to another. In giving someone the power to break you, you become bonded in a way that others are not. Perhaps you are one of those who find you too often make yourself vulnerable to people, but this is a very deliberate act of love and is often difficult for a great number of people. I find it is this sort of deliberate vulnerability that really binds a relationship and seeds love.

Perhaps I would put this — it might be described as honesty — at the heart of love. Upon it I would heap intent, might bind them into intentional honesty, and form this creation into a rose and call it love. Wait, though, it is missing a piece. I might say it is then gentle, no, tender honesty that is pursued with intent, labor, and bravery (for one must be brave to love). I then bind these things together into one emotion and call it love. I apply it in refrain (that is a level of shy fear that is kin to bravery) to everyone who passes me in *agape love*, my intentional willingness to see all people as individuals who are worthy of love by virtue of possessing life in their lungs; and I apply this love with wild (blind even) boldness to those in whom I've invested myself, to whom I've handed the rod and pray they don't beat me with it. And that is what it is to love deliberately.

Allyson White (October 2018)

Loving deliberately... I have struggled with what this means to me since I was asked to write about what it does mean for me. I don't believe that it fits only one person or one type of love. I try to love my children deliberately, my friends and my lover.

For me the most important thing to be able to love deliberately is to be present. To be connected you have to be present. To really listen to what the other person is saying... whether with words or with body language. And if I am distracted and can't be fully present I owe it to that relationship to step back and let them know that I will be there but right now cannot.

Through this struggle I have realized that I am not really present in the relationship I am in. I have to decide whether I can be. There are times I glimpse it but not very often. To be fair to him and myself I need to decide. If on some level I don't believe this is where I belong then how can I ever be fully present? You can love someone and still not be present.. and therefore not loving deliberately.

I am not sure this is the answer you were expecting. I have no wonder words for this. It has made me really look inside. I can say that I do love my children deliberately. And my friends.

I will understand if you cannot use this.
Susan S.

loving deliberately
not only saying your love as often as possible
but also (and more important)
showing your love as much as possible

amelia currently in edinburgh 2017

Part Two

Loving Others ... Deliberately

As I mentioned previously, I believe that we can speak to what loving deliberately is about simply by the *act* of writing about loving – whether it is loving one's country, one's work, other things, or other beings. The following section offers some glimpses of how some contributors go about loving others. Here you will find pieces that are quite familiar and some that you have never seen before. I hope that you enjoy the mix.

LETTER I [From Philip Stanhope, 4th Earl of Chesterfield to his son]

BATH, October 9, O. S. 1746

DEAR BOY: Your distresses in your journey from Heidelberg to Schaffhausen, your lying upon straw, your black bread, and your broken 'berline,' are proper seasonings for the greater fatigues and distresses which you must expect in the course of your travels; and, if one had a mind to moralize, one might call them the samples of the accidents, rubs, and difficulties, which every man meets with in his journey through life. In this journey, the understanding is the 'voiture' that must carry you through; and in proportion as that is stronger or weaker, more or less in repair, your journey will be better or worse; though at best you will now and then find some bad roads, and some bad inns. Take care, therefore, to keep that necessary 'voiture' in perfect good repair; examine, improve, and strengthen it every day: it is in the power, and ought to be the care, of every man to do it; he that neglects it, deserves to feel, and certainly will feel, the fatal effects of that negligence.

'A propos' of negligence: I must say something to you upon that subject. You know I have often told you, that my affection for you was not a weak, womanish one; and, far from blinding me, it makes me but more quick-sighted as to your faults; those it is not only my right, but my duty to tell you of; and it is your duty and your interest to correct them. In the strict scrutiny which I have made into you, I have (thank God) hitherto not discovered any vice of the heart, or any peculiar weakness of the head: but I have discovered laziness, inattention, and indifference; faults which are only pardonable in old men, who, in the decline of life, when health and spirits fail, have a kind of claim to that sort of tranquillity. But a young man should be ambitious to shine, and excel; alert, active, and indefatigable in the means of doing it; and, like Caesar, 'Nil actum reputans, si quid superesset agendum.' You seem to want that 'vivida vis animi,' which spurs and excites most young men to please, to shine, to excel. Without the desire and the pains necessary to be considerable, depend upon it, you never can be so; as, without the desire and attention necessary to please, you never can please. 'Nullum numen abest, si sit prudentia,' is unquestionably true, with regard to everything except poetry; and I am very sure that any man of common understanding may, by proper culture, care, attention, and labor, make himself whatever he pleases, except a good poet. Your destination is the great and busy world; your immediate object is the affairs, the interests, and the history, the constitutions, the customs, and the manners of the several parts of Europe. In this, any man of common sense may, by common application, be sure to excel. Ancient and modern history are, by attention, easily attainable. Geography and chronology the same, none of them requiring any uncommon share of genius or invention. Speaking and Writing, clearly, correctly, and with ease and grace, are certainly to be acquired, by reading the best authors with care, and by attention to the best living models. These are the qualifications more particularly necessary for you, in your department, which you may be possessed of, if you please; and which, I tell you fairly, I shall be very angry at you, if you are not; because, as you have the means in your hands, it will be your own fault only.

If care and application are necessary to the acquiring of those qualifications, without which you can never be considerable, nor make a figure in the world, they are not less necessary with regard to the lesser accomplishments, which are requisite to make you agreeable and pleasing in society. In truth, whatever is worth doing at all, is worth doing well; and nothing can be done well without attention: I therefore carry the necessity of attention down to the lowest things, even to dancing and dress. Custom has made dancing sometimes necessary for a young man; therefore mind it while you learn it that you may learn to do it well, and not be ridiculous, though in a ridiculous act. Dress is of the same nature; you must dress; therefore attend to it; not in order to rival or to excel a fop in it, but in order to avoid singularity, and consequently ridicule. Take great care always to be dressed like the reasonable people of your own age, in the place where you are; whose dress is never spoken of one way or another, as either too negligent or too much studied.

What is commonly called an absent man, is commonly either a very weak, or a very affected man; but be he which he will, he is, I am sure, a very disagreeable man in company. He fails in all the common offices of civility; he seems not to know those people to-day, whom yesterday he appeared to live in intimacy with. He takes no part in the general conversation; but, on the contrary, breaks into it from time to time, with some start of his own, as if he waked from a dream. This (as I said before) is a sure indication, either of a mind so weak that it is not able to bear above one object at a time; or so affected, that it would be supposed to be wholly engrossed by, and directed to, some very great and important objects. Sir Isaac Newton, Mr. Locke, and (it may be) five or six more, since the creation of the world, may have had a right to absence, from that intense thought which the things they were investigating required. But if a young man, and a man of the world, who has no such avocations to plead, will claim and exercise that right of absence in company, his pretended right should, in my mind, be turned into an involuntary absence, by his perpetual exclusion out of company. However frivolous a company may be, still, while you are among them, do not show them, by your inattention, that you think them so; but rather take their tone, and conform in some degree to their weakness, instead of manifesting your contempt for them. There is nothing that people bear more impatiently, or forgive less, than contempt; and an injury is much sooner forgotten than an insult. If, therefore, you would rather please than offend, rather be well than ill spoken of, rather be loved than hated; remember to have that constant attention about you which flatters every man's little vanity; and the want of which, by mortifying his pride, never fails to excite his resentment, or at least his ill will. For instance, most people (I might say all people) have their weaknesses; they have their aversions and their likings, to such or such things; so that, if you were to laugh at a man for his aversion to a cat, or cheese (which are common antipathies), or, by inattention and negligence, to let them come in his way, where you could prevent it, he would, in the first case, think himself insulted, and, in the second, slighted, and would remember both. Whereas your care to procure for him what he likes, and to remove from him what he hates, shows him that he is at least an object of your attention; flatters his vanity, and makes him possibly more your friend, than a more important service would have done. With regard to women, attentions still below these are necessary, and, by the custom of the world, in some measure due, according to the laws of good-breeding.

My long and frequent letters, which I send you, in great doubt of their success, put me in mind of certain papers, which you have very lately, and I formerly, sent up to kites, along the string, which we called messengers; some of them the wind used to blow away, others were torn by the string, and but few of them got up and stuck to the kite. But I will content myself now, as I did then, if some of my present messengers do but stick to you. Adieu!

The Good-Morrow

I wonder by my troth, what thou and I
Did, till we loved? Were we not wean'd till then?
But suck'd on country pleasures, childishly?
Or snorted we in the Seven Sleepers' den?
'Twas so; but this, all pleasures fancies be;
If ever any beauty I did see,
Which I desired, and got, 'twas but a dream of thee.

And now good-morrow to our waking souls,
Which watch not one another out of fear;
For love all love of other sights controls,
And makes one little room an everywhere.
Let sea-discoverers to new worlds have gone;
Let maps to other, worlds on worlds have shown;
Let us possess one world; each hath one, and is one.

My face in thine eye, thine in mine appears,
And true plain hearts do in the faces rest;

Where can we find two better hemispheres
Without sharp north, without declining west?
Whatever dies, was not mix'd equally;
If our two loves be one, or thou and I
Love so alike that none can slacken, none can die.

John Donne (1572 – 1631)

Loving Deliberately in Time
Bob Ekelund

I would imagine that most people believe that "loving deliberately" requires knowledge of the thing or person loved. I realize that there is no love without some deliberation but I experienced an astonishing exception at a party one night thirty-five years ago. It was for incoming doctoral students, one of whom kept sneaking glances my way. I, a full professor, remember leaning over to tell a friend – "see that guy over there – I'm going to spend the rest of my life with him!" (My friend guffawed and she, who has never told a lie, remembers it to this day). I knew I was in love.

I have often wondered at these uncharacteristic bold feelings. The word "love" is often misused. I "love" fried chicken, gardening and Claude Debussy's music, but is that a deliberate love? Then there is lust – often confused with love – which is actually little more than an evolutionary imperative for survival. Some would say that lust that leads to love, but in most cases I doubt that. Lust generally leads to more lust. I was and am firm, as was Thoreau, in my belief that only knowledge *can* lead to love. "Love at first sight" is most almost always a manifestation of lustful attraction. My experience may have contained lust but I maintain to this day that it was essentially love – and a love without full knowledge.

No, what happened to me that fateful night was falling in love without deliberation; OK, with a little lust in it. But then, there must be more to deliberated love than just "knowledge" for I had never met or spoke to Mark. How could this be? First let me say that "loving deliberately" means (at least to me and possibly Thoreau) just what the words mean. It is a conscious and deliberate act of the will – but one where *length* of deliberations is variable. How many times I have hated a poem or a piece of music (a certain Bach prelude I worked on recently), often for a long period of time, only to finally understand and love its beauty and/or profundity. (That doesn't mean that I'll ever love the music of John Cage, but who knows).

Surely, knowledge and understanding are critical parts of loving deliberately. And Thoreau's desired reduction of attention to only the "essential facts of life" and his idea that love was a learning process indicates that his desire to love deliberately *has a time dimension*. Ordinarily we cannot love what we do not know – be it a person, music, science, art, or nature or anything we are curious and seek to learn about. I am deliberately hesitant to do otherwise and do so only in the rarest of circumstances.

What happened to me at that party? No real deliberation. No real knowledge. No acute interchange. No nothing. No entertaining possible problems, such as a significant age difference, as I drank another martini. But love was there and I was determined, in spite of the knotty problems, that it would become a deliberate love for him as well. How could I love without knowledge of the thing (this time a person) loved. *My* quandary lasted for several years as I brought him into my life and finally revealed my heart. He had to find deliberate love and I had to gain knowledge so that I could, with Thoreau, "discover that I had lived."

Then it dawned on me – perhaps "loving deliberately" has a deeper meaning than knowledge – that is, perhaps what is loved is a *reflection* of our own deepest feelings about life, inanimate objects and the universe, not only a person. That process is mysterious, fundamental and non-verbal – a process best carried on in private ("in "the woods") but, I think, not necessarily so. Solitude may be willed to oneself anywhere – in Times Square or a teeming Shanghai street. To love deliberately is to carry within us love for people, for nature, as Thoreau did, or for music or art or bowling. Nature is completely independent of truth and morality – that lies within ourselves. Love is always ours to take or leave or *independently to accept* – that is the deliberate choice. Maybe that view might help explain rare instances of "love at first sight." For the longest time, love does not exist. Then, suddenly, there is deliberate love – often non-verbal and a personal choice that lasts for a short time or, in my case, more than three decades. Is it magic? No, it is a rational choice we make for ourselves.

Loving Bob Deliberately
Mark Thornton

I made a very deliberate choice in 1982. I would leave New York and the "normal life" and move to Alabama, of all places, to become an economist. Most people thought I was crazy, but I had come of age during the 1970s. It was the time of inflation, recession, gas lines, Watergate, losing the Vietnam War, and Disco. My last two years of college as an undergraduate, America had 10% unemployment and 18% interest rates. I wanted know why and how to fix it.

At a cocktail party for incoming graduate students I met the people who would populate and one who would change my new life. Meeting so many likeminded individuals was great, but the most interesting person for me was Bob. He was sharply dressed and seemed to me the life of the party. He was my focus.

At that time, I was not thinking of love or lust. That just wasn't me. After all, as a Yankee, agnostic, anarcho-capitalist, I was not going to come out of the closet on my first day in the heart of the conservative, religious, and "patriotic" South! I barely had the nerve to tell people I was raised Roman Catholic!

The next couple of years were hard, but I loved the dynamic camaraderie of the faculty and students in the basement of Thach Hall at Auburn University. After I had finished my coursework, I began to work with Bob on things like one of his new books and painting his house. We partied together. We wrote together. We started a relationship together, deliberately. We may have known each other better than we knew ourselves back then and I knew Love for the first time.

I have continued to love Bob more *deliberately* over time.

I don't think it is something you either have or not, but it is something that grows with knowledge over time. It has for me and, after more than thirty years, we continue to *build* our life together in remarkable ways.

Defeated by Love

The sky was lit by the splendor of the moon
So powerful I fell to the ground.
Your Love has made me sure
I am ready to forsake this worldly Life
And surrender to the magnificence of your Being.

Rumi (1207 – 1273)

Loving Deliberately

We've all got that one place we always return to. For me, it's the diner on the south side of town. Perhaps you prefer a bistro downtown or that worn down old steakhouse near the airport. Regardless, we all have one. It's comfortable and steady, the decor never changes, and at least one of the waitresses has been there since what feels like the dawn of time. When you walk in the doors of your favorite restaurant it evokes the feeling of coming home.

You sit down with the menu and peruse. Nothing has been updated in years, but still you scan to see if, maybe, something new has snuck its way onto the sticky, worn pages. If you're anything like me, you'll spend a moment considering all the options of what you could have. Could it be the BLT? Perhaps you'll spring for the fish and chips today. But why risk it on something new when you could go with a tried and true option? For me, the classic cheeseburger and fries never fails to satisfy.

And that's usually how it goes. Not just when you're having lunch, but also in life. Humans are creatures of habit. We continue to make the same choices time after time. Not because we necessarily enjoy the results of those choices, but because we know the results. And when our usual choice isn't available, we tend to opt for the most reliable outcome. It's the same way in love. We want to make relationship choices that serve our best interests, however, we find ourselves making the same choices because the unknown is more frightening than the reality we are accustomed to.

When I was in my early twenties, I had a tendency to passively break off my relationships. If things were progressing the way I wanted it was easier to disappear, or find a way to offend my partner, than to openly tell that person I didn't want to be with them. It was a tried and true method, and the only way I felt comfortable moving on. The last time I had this notion was several years ago. On the surface, my boyfriend at the time was great. But at just over a year into our relationship I was starting to feel stifled. My nights alone had lessened, we starting to meet each other's families, and worst of all, he was subtly pushing me to become a better version of myself. After a lifetime of poor relationships and even worse relationship role models, these behaviors just weren't in my game plan. Inevitably, I fell back to my usual cycle. I stopped calling and texting him, but he'd still come over. I would spend late nights drinking at the bar, not coming home until well after the bar had closed, but he was always there to help me nurse a hangover the next morning. It seemed like no matter what I did, he wasn't going to budge.

On a late winter night, I set up what I thought would be my relationship breaking magnum opus. Having invited a particularly seedy group of characters over to my house I knew that my boyfriend would surely be pissed upon coming home. We were drinking and engaging in a few not-necessarily-legal activities when he came home. And this time I could tell I had broken him. He was silent. Angry silent. His breath grew heavy and small slits replaced the usually soft brown eyes. Judging glances were thrown at everyone in the group and he finally landed on me.

"You know you shouldn't be doing that," he said.

I stared at him for a moment and then turned to continue a conversation I had been having with my friend. For the rest of the night he sat there, with gritted teeth, watching as people left one by one, eventually leaving just the two of us alone together. It was the moment I had been waiting for, the tumultuous fight that would surely be the end of the relationship I could no longer manage. Instead, he got up and went to bed.

In the morning, he gave me a hug, told me he loved me, and left for work. Over the next few months this never changed. I would try to push him away, but he would always pull me closer and remind that love was there. Eventually, my ability to push grew weaker, and the realization that perhaps I did deserve that love grew stronger. It was a slow progression, but it was steady. At some point I had forgotten my yearnings for independence and was fostering new emotions. Emotions, that made me want to stay.

It was his way of loving deliberately that allowed me to grow as a person. In the course of our seven-year relationship, that is still continuing to this day, I have been able to return the favor of deliberately loving him. We don't always like each other. In fact, there have been times when you could say we hated each other. But there has always been a thread, however small, of love that joins us together. It's kind of like that classic cheeseburger and fries. Somedays the meat is undercooked and the fries are burnt. That won't keep me from ordering it every time. Even if it's bad today I will make the same choice; because it's reliable and I know that chances are it's going to be better tomorrow.

Tricia Wickens
December 2018

How do I love thee? Let me count the ways.

I love thee to the depth and breadth and height
My soul can reach, when feeling out of sight
For the ends of Being and ideal Grace.
I love thee to the level of everyday's
Most quiet need, by sun and candlelight.
I love thee freely, as men might strive for right;
I love thee purely, as they turn from praise.
I love thee with the passion put to use
In my old griefs, and with my childhood's faith.
I love thee with a love I seemed to lose
With my lost saints, - I love thee with the breath,
Smiles, and tears, of all my life!-and, if God choose,
I shall but love thee better after death.

Elizabeth Barrett Browning 1850

Connecting

My young legs carried me across a thin stream,
Where I took in the blue sky and the thick summer air from the other side.
I felt alive.

A folded note opened me up to a short hallway romance,
And I searched to understand new and uncharted feelings.
I felt acceptance.

I saw a different future arrive at the end of an aisle,
And I've smiled at where those years together have taken me.
I felt hope.

As I cradled something both incredible and small,
I searched across his face for a common thread to my soul.
I felt purpose.

And as I now open the doors to let those parts of me go,
I know a departure can mean the arrival of new experiences.
I feel fulfilled.

When you feel alive, accept, and have a sense of hope, purpose and fulfillment, your soul is giving you lessons on how to connect.

Because when you connect with whatever helps to make you whole…you are loving deliberately.

Ray Allston

Beethoven's Love Letter

July 6th, in the morning
My angel, my all, my very self. – Only a few words today, and, what is more, written in pencil (and with your pencil)–I shan't be certain of my rooms here until tomorrow; what an unnecessary waste of time is all this–Why this profound sorrow, when necessity speaks–can our love endure without sacrifices, without our demanding everything from one another, can you alter the fact that you are not wholly mine, that I am not wholly yours?–Dear God, look at Nature in all her beauty and set your heart at rest about what must be–Love demands all, and rightly so, and thus it is for me with you, for you with me– but you forget so easily that I must live for me and for you; if we were completely united, you would fee this painful necessity just as little as I do–My journey was dreadful and I did not arrive here until yesterday at four o'clock in the morning. As there were few horses the mail coach chose another route, but what a dreadful road it was; at the last state but one I was warned not to travel by night; attempts were made to frighten me about a forest, but all this only spurred me on to proceed–and it was wrong of me to do so.. The coach broke down, of course, owing to the dreadful road which had not been made up and was nothing but a country track. If we hadn't had those two postillions I should have been left stranded on the way– On the other ordinary road Esterhazy with eight horses met with the same fate as I did with four–Yet I felt to a certain extent that pleasure I always feel when I have overcome some difficulty successfully–Well, let me turn quickly from outer to inner experiences. No doubt we shall meet soon; and today also time fails me to tell you of the thoughts which during these last few days I have been revolving about my life–If our hearts were always closely united, I would certainly entertain no such thoughts. My heart overflows

with a longing to tell you so many things—Oh—there are moments when I find that speech is quite inadequate—Be cheerful— and be for ever my faithful, my only sweetheart, my all, as I am yours. The gods must send us everything else, whatever must and shall be our fate—
Your faithful Ludwig

Monday evening, July 6th
You are suffering, you, my most precious one—I have noticed the very moment that letters have to be handed in very early, on Monday—or on Thursday—the only days when the mail coach goes from here to K[arlsbad].—You are suffering—Oh, where I am, you are with me—I will see to it that you and I, that I can live with you. What a life!!!! as it is now!!!! without you—pursued by the kindness of people here and there, a kindness that I think—that I wish to deserve just as little as I deserve it—man's homage to man—that pains me—and when I consider myself in the setting of the universe, what I am and what is the man—whom one calls the greatest of me—and yet—on the other hand therein lies the divine element in man—I weep when I think that probably you will not receive the first news of me until Saturday—However much you love me—good night—Since I am taking the baths I must get off to sleep—Dear God—so near! so far! Is not our love truly founded in heaven—and, what is more, as strongly cemented as the firmament of Heaven?—

Good morning, on July 7th
Even when I am in bed my thoughts rush to you, my eternally beloved, now and then joyfully, then again sadly, waiting to know whether Fate will hear our prayer—To face life I must live altogether with you or never see you. Yes, I am resolved to be a wanderer abroad until I can fly to your arms and say that I have

found my true home with you and enfolded in your arms can let my soul be wafted to the realm on blessed spirits—alas, unfortunately it must be so—You will become composed, the more so as you know that I am faithful to you; no other woman can ever possess my heart—never—never—Oh God, why must one be separated from her who is so dear. Yet my life in V[ienna] at present is a miserable life—Your love has made me both the happiest and the unhappiest of mortals—At my age I now need stability and regularity in my life—can this coexist with our relationship?—Angel, I have just heard that the post goes every day—and therefore I must close, so that you may receive the letter immediately—Be calm; for only by calmly considering our lives can we achieve our purpose to live together—Be calm—love me—Today—yesterday—what tearful longing for you—for you—you—my life—my all—all good wishes to you—Oh, do continue to love me—never misjudge your lover's most faithful heart.

ever yours
ever mine
ever ours

L.

Note: This letter to Beethoven's Immortal Beloved was found after the composer died in 1827. The identity of his love has never been determined with certainty.

If ever two were one, then surely we.
If ever man were loved by wife, then thee.
If ever wife was happy in a man,
Compare with me, ye women, if you can.
I prize thy love more than whole mines of gold,
Or all the riches that the East doth hold.
My love is such that rivers cannot quench,
Nor ought but love from thee give recompense.
Thy love is such I can no way repay;
The heavens reward thee manifold, I pray.
Then while we live, in love let's so persever,
That when we live no more, we may live ever.

Anne Bradstreet
(1612-1672)

5/23/16
Loving Deliberately, my story.

Steve:

Here's my memory of an event that falls in the category of Loving Deliberately. It was 1977 and I was living in Denver with my girlfriend, Lois. We had lived together for two years and knew each other's personalities and quirks well. We had been to couples counseling to work on our relationship. I was having doubts about the viability of relationship and thinking about breaking it off, even though we had a strong connection. I was working as a land surveyor for a private Civil Engineering firm. The work was interesting, mentally stimulating, and I loved working outdoors. I applied for a new job with the Federal Government (U.S. Geological Survey) who was hiring land surveyors for a special project. The project was to perform boundary surveys for all of the National Parks. The work would involve 100% travel and the opportunity to see all of the National Parks. It was my dream job! It was when I was offered the job that I had to think deeply and hard about what mattered more to me, my dream job or my relationship with Lois. I could hear the Lovin' Spoonful singing "Did you ever have to make up your mind?" in my head. I made a decision to stay with my girlfriend and walk away from my dream job. It was a difficult, even painful, decision but one that I don't regret. After some detours through grad school (me) and medical school (her), we were married in 1981. We have two grown sons and a loving relationship.

Best Regards,
Jerry

A Glimpse

A GLIMPSE, through an interstice caught,
Of a crowd of workmen and drivers in a bar-room, around the stove, late of a winter night—And I unremark'd seated in a corner;
Of a youth who loves me, and whom I love, silently approaching, and seating himself near, that he may hold me by the hand;
A long while, amid the noises of coming and going—of drinking and oath and smutty jest,
There we two, content, happy in being together, speaking little, perhaps not a word.

Walt Whitman

Flashback Fragments of Friendship
By Elissa Alden

I bask in warm memories of fleeting youth,
Youth we were so eager to run from,
Not comprehending the charm—
We always danced.

Merry crooked driveway cartwheels,
All night stay ups,
Tareyton drivebys,
Shadowland drama with perfect hair,
Rest room meet ups to rectify unwanted proof of dalliances—
And still we danced

Cherry Herring sleepovers,
Ham and cheese delights,
Tears and crushes Blowin' in the wind,
Frantic phone calls,
Unspeakable heartbreak weathered hand and hand—
Dancing as ever.

Accidents (real and feigned),
Eye shadow bruises and Silent Night girl scouts,
Emergency room cigarettes,
Weddings, Babies, Funerals—
Did we still dance?

Don Ho,
Road trips,
Chinatown glee,
Rubberband hair,

Knee socks,
Hospital dormitory with warm blankets—
A lifetime of laughter measured with endless dance steps.

Thank-you.

>   For Barb on #65

Falling Stars
Rainer Maria Rilke

Do you remember still the falling stars
that like swift horses through the heavens raced
and suddenly leaped across the hurdles of our wishes? Do you recall?
And we did make so many! For there were countless numbers of stars:
each time we looked above we were astounded by the swiftness of their daring play,
while in our hearts we felt safe and secure
watching these brilliant bodies disintegrate,
knowing somehow we had survived their fall.

Steve,

Loving Deliberately

Remember how in their first apartment
they only had that fresh-from-ikea bed
to rest their bodies on? He was husband,
a brand new one, body-rubbing his wife
under their checkered duvet, television
not yet there to distract them from the cold.

Though to be fair, the Los Angeles cold
couldn't quite fit in their small apartment,
newly-wed full and all. The television
came with Christmas, slanted to face the bed
and new couch at once. Remember the wife,
how she'd shoulder rub with her husband

over the little steel stove, her husband
chopping the garlic, broccoli getting cold
in its tinfoil blanket, elbows knocking. That wife,
she made a restaurant of their apartment
that first year, a dining room of their bed.
They even forgot the television

was there some nights—who needs television
with newly-wed teeth flashing, with a husband
as funny as him to make a stage of their bed?
Though I wish they'd known laughter could still turn cold
for mated souls. Heaven's not that apartment
where one first steps on the feelings of his wife

with clumsy twenty-something feet, his wife
fiddling with her ring. The television
rounded out the silence of their apartment
on those days when she avoided her husband's
glance, or he avoided hers. It got cold,
that space between their bodies on the bed,

and gets cold still, their stained-ikea bed,
but less, and less, and less, because, my wife,
they laid out their instructions on the cold
floor, of deliberate love, as the television
helped them to laugh, their knees aching. As husband
and wife, they built a home from an apartment,

pieced together the bed, the television,
the bodies, young bodies—wife and husband
against the cold, assembled that first apartment.

Josh

Shakespeare's Sonnet #130

My mistress' eyes are nothing like the sun;
Coral is far more red than her lips' red;
If snow be white, why then her breasts are dun;
If hairs be wires, black wires grow on her head.
I have seen roses damasked, red and white,
But no such roses see I in her cheeks;
And in some perfumes is there more delight
Than in the breath that from my mistress reeks.
I love to hear her speak, yet well I know
That music hath a far more pleasing sound;
I grant I never saw a goddess go;
My mistress when she walks treads on the ground.
    And yet, by heaven, I think my love as rare
    As any she belied with false compare.

Loving My Children Deliberately

Loving deliberately is a cut above. It is the love I have for my three children. They are more important to me than my faith, what I do to make a living, my friends, my other family members and myself.

Yet all of the people and things other than my children that I love are related somehow, maybe in my love for them, a love which is intense and important but a cut below my love for my children whom I love with all I can give … all ways. They have my full attention, which means I am there for them always, but always with no smothering, never smothering. This is very difficult to do, of course, and my very favourite challenge each and every day.

Ben from BC
December 2018

Loving deliberately goes hand in hand with forgiveness. If your child hurts you, it's impossible to not forgive them if you love them deliberately. Even if they caused you great pain, you never let go of a mother's love. You may want to hate them for what they said or did, but what is hate? A cancer that grows inside you. It doesn't hurt them, only you. So we must love our children no matter what age they are, from infants to adulthood. It's easy to forgive a small child but harder when they're an adult. We must love them deliberately ... always, with no "buts" for what they might have said or done. With that kind of love goes forgiveness. Like hate, not forgiving someone only eats you up inside. It doesn't affect the other person. But by forgiving them it gives you peace. So, forgive, love deliberately, because one day that child will call you and act like nothing had happened all that time ago. He'll call with some great news and you'll be happy for him and all will be well again.

Gisela

It was many and many a year ago,
    In a kingdom by the sea,
That a maiden there lived whom you may know
    By the name of Annabel Lee;
And this maiden she lived with no other thought
    Than to love and be loved by me.

I was a child and *she* was a child,
    In this kingdom by the sea,
But we loved with a love that was more than love—
    I and my Annabel Lee—
With a love that the wingèd seraphs of Heaven
    Coveted her and me.

And this was the reason that, long ago,
    In this kingdom by the sea,
A wind blew out of a cloud, chilling
    My beautiful Annabel Lee;
So that her highborn kinsmen came
    And bore her away from me,
To shut her up in a sepulchre
    In this kingdom by the sea.

The angels, not half so happy in Heaven,
    Went envying her and me—
Yes!—that was the reason (as all men know,
    In this kingdom by the sea)
That the wind came out of the cloud by night,
    Chilling and killing my Annabel Lee.

But our love it was stronger by far than the love
    Of those who were older than we—
    Of many far wiser than we—
And neither the angels in Heaven above
    Nor the demons down under the sea
Can ever dissever my soul from the soul
    Of the beautiful Annabel Lee;

For the moon never beams, without bringing me dreams
    Of the beautiful Annabel Lee;
And the stars never rise, but I feel the bright eyes
    Of the beautiful Annabel Lee;
And so, all the night-tide, I lie down by the side
    Of my darling—my darling—my life and my bride,
    In her sepulchre there by the sea—
    In her tomb by the sounding sea.

E. A. Poe

Loving Deliberately

Loving my family, my close friends, my work, my Spiritual Center, my self is not difficult; nor does it take deliberation. It is simple and pleasant. I am very good at this without taking extra effort to do so.

The sort of Love that must be done deliberately (and requires enormous strength, dedication, and effort) is the love that I work hard at having for those who wish me harm, people who regard themselves as my enemy (whether they know me or not, whether I know them or not), unpleasant, mean-spirited, negative, angry, aggressive, cruel people. You get the idea. I am not always successful at summoning up deliberate Love for these individuals, but I do make the attempt – deliberately. And I am grateful for my ability to care enough to do so.

Anonymously submitted by a Friend who is an American expat living in Hong Kong (late 2017)

O Deus, Ego Amo Te
by *Gerard Manley Hopkins*

O God, I love thee, I love thee —
Not out of hope of heaven for me
Nor fearing not to love and be
In the everlasting burning.
Thou, thou, my Jesus, after me
Didst reach thine arms out dying,
For my sake sufferedst nails and lance, —
Mocked and marred countenance,
Sorrows passing number,
Sweat and care and cumber,
Yea and death, and this for me,
And thou couldst see me sinning:
Then I, why should not I love thee,
Jesu so much in love with me?
Not for heaven's sake; not to be
Out of hell by loving thee;
Not for any gains I see;
But just the way that thou didst me
I do love and I will love thee:
What must I love thee, Lord, for then? —
For being my king and God. Amen.

Part Three

Loving a Place ... Deliberately

Only three entries here, but I think that you will agree with me that this section and the pieces within it need a place of their own. Yet, they really are so closely tied with all of the others....

*Chicago**

> Hog Butcher for the World,
> Tool maker, Stacker of Wheat,
> Player with Railroads and the Nation's
>   Freight Handler;
> Stormy, husky, brawling,
> City of the Big Shoulders:

They tell me you are wicked and I believe them, for I have seen your painted women under the gas lamps luring the farm boys.

And they tell me you are crooked and I answer: yes, it is true I have seen the gunman kill and go free to kill again.

And they tell me you are brutal and my reply is: On the faces of women and children I have seen the marks of wanton hunger.

And having answered so I turn once more to those who sneer at this my city, and I give them back the sneer and say to them:

Come and show me another city with lifted head singing so proud to be alive and coarse and strong and cunning.

Flinging magnetic curses amid the toil of piling job on job, here is a tall bold slugger set vivid against the little soft cities;

Fierce as a dog with tongue lapping for action, cunning as a savage pitted against the wilderness,

---

* I have included this wonderful poem because it is simply a must in this anthology and with a tip of the cap to Studs Terkel – born in New York City but a deliberate lover of The Windy City.

> Bareheaded,
> Shoveling,
> Wrecking,
> Planning,
> Building, breaking, rebuilding,

Under the smoke, dust all over his mouth, laughing with white teeth,

Under the terrible burden of destiny laughing as a young man laughs,

Laughing even as an ignorant fighter laughs who has never lost a battle,

Bragging and laughing that under his wrist is the pulse, and under his ribs the heart of the people,

> Laughing!

Laughing the stormy, husky, brawling laughter of Youth, half-naked, sweating, proud to be Hog Butcher, Tool Maker, Stacker of Wheat, Player with Railroads and Freight Handler to the Nation.

Carl Sandburg

Hey bud here goes my take on Loving Deliberately as related to my travel business.

There is something to be said about Loving Deliberately as related to how I view my travel company and the many clients we send all over this amazing Earth. To say I love my job is a large understatement. When you have passion for something everything you do surrounding that passion is carefully thought out. Everything I do for my clients is always done with a conscious and intentional action and purpose. My main destination of emphasis is Africa, due to my endless passion for the life changing experiences she grants us. When I begin to plan a new trip for a client who has never stepped foot on the African continent my juices begin to flow. I go into my glass blowing mindset where the smallest imperfection becomes the largest object of succeeding. I will sometimes put on a certain genre of music to get my mind tuned in with fierce focus and patience. For this becomes a act of love for me and my center of gravity as a human is again fulfilled with the greatest joy we can possess and that is happiness. To say there are no coincidences in life means you have to believe in a power greater than yourself which I do. To feel the purpose of your life every day is a gift not everyone is given. My life experiences have taken me to places I never thought I'd visit. Those same experiences have led me to meet people I would not otherwise have met, like Steve Bannow. My love for Africa is deeply rooted within my soul and is a feeling hard to explain sometimes. I do know that my never ending passion for what I do lifts me up to a higher place in my heart, with my family, with my friends and with my clients. All of that positive energy comes from Loving Deliberately.

Hope that is ok. You can add anything you feel is worthy based on our friendship and business relationship we have formed over many years now.

Mark Gerling

I went to the woods because I wished to live deliberately, to front only the essential facts of life, and see if I could not learn what it had to teach, and not, when I came to die, discover that I had not lived. I did not wish to live what was not life, living is so dear; nor did I wish to practice resignation, unless it was quite necessary. I wanted to live deep and suck out all the marrow of life, to live so sturdily and Spartan-like as to put to rout all that was not life, to cut a broad swath and shave close, to drive life into a corner, and reduce it to its lowest terms....

– Henry David Thoreau

Part Four

Loving Work ... Deliberately

Those who love work deliberately do not necessarily do so above and beyond others and other things in their lives. It is just that for some of us extraordinarily lucky folks loving what we *do* is a huge part of loving what and who we *are*.

I love life fundamentally.
I love my family unconditionally.
I love my work *deliberately*.
My work requires a unique sort of focus, a unique sort of discipline, a unique sort of passion, a unique sort of dedication. I cannot describe what exactly makes my relationship to my work, my love for my work, unique. It just is.
And so, I love my work *deliberately*.

Kim
Denver 2017

Robert Frost's "After Apple-Picking"

My long two-pointed ladder's sticking through a tree
Toward heaven still,
And there's a barrel that I didn't fill
Beside it, and there may be two or three
Apples I didn't pick upon some bough.
But I am done with apple-picking now.
Essence of winter sleep is on the night,
The scent of apples: I am drowsing off.
I cannot rub the strangeness from my sight
I got from looking through a pane of glass
I skimmed this morning from the drinking trough
And held against the world of hoary grass.
It melted, and I let it fall and break.
But I was well
Upon my way to sleep before it fell,
And I could tell
What form my dreaming was about to take.
Magnified apples appear and disappear,
Stem end and blossom end,
And every fleck of russet showing clear.
My instep arch not only keeps the ache,
It keeps the pressure of a ladder-round.
I feel the ladder sway as the boughs bend.
And I keep hearing from the cellar bin
The rumbling sound
Of load on load of apples coming in.
For I have had too much
Of apple-picking: I am overtired
Of the great harvest I myself desired.
There were ten thousand thousand fruit to touch,

Cherish in hand, lift down, and not let fall.
For all
That struck the earth,
No matter if not bruised or spiked with stubble,
Went surely to the cider-apple heap
As of no worth.
One can see what will trouble
This sleep of mine, whatever sleep it is.
Were he not gone,
The woodchuck could say whether it's like his
Long sleep, as I describe its coming on,
Or just some human sleep.

I am 33 and some people might think I am lonely.
They would be mistaken.
You see, I have not fathered any of my own children and I do not have a spouse or even a partner at the moment. Nevertheless, I am anything *but* lonely.
I am very much in Love and I am actively, *deliberately* very much in Love.
The object of my love is more important than anything except Life….

I am a teacher.

Jack
Arlington 2018

As Above, So Below

"… All things are interrelated. As above, so below. We are fragments of an unutterable whole. Meaning is always in search of itself. Unsuspected revelations await us around the next corner."
  —Charles Simic, "Street-Corner Theology" from Dime-Store Alchemy

On my last day of work Donny called
to say he was not going to make it to his
psychiatrist appointment even though he
was only one El stop away.

The problem, he said, was people thought
he wanted to push them all off the platform,
but he knew they, actually, wanted to push
him in front of one of these express trains
screaming past the wooden platform
between locals.

*

The upstairs neighbors said their girl
practices for active shooters in school
by running into the bathroom and standing
on the toilet so her shoes aren't visible
under the stall door.

*

The shell grows, following the laws of sacred
geometry when left untouched.

The hive destroyed, the bees followed the queen to
the trunk of a 1996 Chevy Cavalier.

The plants in my office curl toward the sun and
every week I move the chopsticks holding the jade
upright, struggling to create some order
during a cancelled hour.

*

There's a yellow-curbed strip of garden outside my window
where Hector the building engineer took two bunnies from
an orange bucket and released them into the dirt
between the sidewalk and the street as he didn't want
to soak them while watering.

A magic trick – I hadn't noticed him scoop them
up in the first place.

*

After finishing a conspiracy theory poem about how
the federal government killed a famous athlete's father
to protect the price of another historical sports figure's
baseball card, I ran into the same man who illuminated
those links, the racist plots of 3 AM talk radio and the
manifest class system which keeps the invisible hand
feeding the devil.

On the El platform, the man and his girlfriend introduced
themselves politely in case I had forgotten. I had to prove
I remembered where they lived after he, released by the state,
finished his Not Guilty by Reason of Insanity adjudication and
upon his return to the world, the opulence of the cereal aisle
provoked a panic attack and a demand to return to the unit.

Proud we all remembered each others' names,
they, somewhat disappointed, told me I should be
driving a Porsche, not riding the train.

*

Anxiety is the gap between the way things are
and the way we want them to be.

The tip of the iceberg is the only known quantity
and all symptoms are an effort
to keep us alive.

Zak Mucha
Chicago
January 2018

I Hear America Singing

I hear America singing, the varied carols I hear,
Those of mechanics, each one singing his as it should be blithe and strong,
The carpenter singing his as he measures his plank or beam,
The mason singing his as he makes ready for work, or leaves off work,
The boatman singing what belongs to him in his boat, the deckhand singing on the steamboat deck,
The shoemaker singing as he sits on his bench, the hatter singing as he stands,
The wood-cutter's song, the ploughboy's on his way in the morning, or at noon intermission or at sundown,
The delicious singing of the mother, or of the young wife at work, or of the girl sewing or washing,
Each singing what belongs to him or her and to none else,
The day what belongs to the day—at night the party of young fellows, robust, friendly,
Singing with open mouths their strong melodious songs.

Walt Whitman

Part Five

Loving One's Country
... Deliberately

It may seem odd that the love letter that follows immediately – one of the most profound that I have ever read – would appear in a section of this book titled "Loving One's *Country* ... Deliberately." The fact of the matter is that Sullivan Ballou loved his wife very deeply and he also loved his sons and his prosperous legal career and his life. Yet he was willing to risk everything in defense of his country and its great promise. Yes, this letter could appear just about any place in this book, but I have made my decision. I sincerely believe that Major Ballou and his wife, Sarah, would understand.

July the 14th, 1861
Washington D.C.

My very dear Sarah:
The indications are very strong that we shall move in a few days—perhaps tomorrow. Lest I should not be able to write you again, I feel impelled to write lines that may fall under your eye when I shall be no more.

Our movement may be one of a few days duration and full of pleasure—and it may be one of severe conflict and death to me. Not my will, but thine O God, be done. If it is necessary that I should fall on the battlefield for my country, I am ready. I have no misgivings about, or lack of confidence in, the cause in which I am engaged, and my courage does not halt or falter. I know how strongly American Civilization now leans upon the triumph of the Government, and how great a debt we owe to those who went before us through the blood and suffering of the Revolution. And I am willing—perfectly willing—to lay down all my joys in this life, to help maintain this Government, and to pay that debt.

But, my dear wife, when I know that with my own joys I lay down nearly all of yours, and replace them in this life with cares and sorrows—when, after having eaten for long years the bitter fruit of orphanage myself, I must offer it as their only sustenance to my dear little children—is it weak or dishonorable, while the banner of my purpose floats calmly and proudly in the breeze, that my unbounded love for you, my darling wife and children, should struggle in fierce, though useless, contest with my love of country.

Sarah, my love for you is deathless, it seems to bind me to you with mighty cables that nothing but Omnipotence could break; and yet my love of Country comes over me like a strong wind and bears me irresistibly on with all these chains to the battlefield.

The memories of the blissful moments I have spent with you come creeping over me, and I feel most gratified to God and to you that I have enjoyed them so long. And hard it is for me to give them up and burn to ashes the hopes of future years, when God willing, we might still have lived and loved together and seen our sons grow up to honorable manhood around us. I have, I know, but few and small claims upon Divine Providence, but something whispers to me—perhaps it is the wafted prayer of my little Edgar—that I shall return to my loved ones unharmed. If I do not, my dear Sarah, never forget how much I love you, and when my last breath escapes me on the battlefield, it will whisper your name.

Forgive my many faults, and the many pains I have caused you. How thoughtless and foolish I have often been! How gladly would I wash out with my tears every little spot upon your happiness, and struggle with all the misfortune of this world, to shield you and my children from harm. But I cannot. I must watch you from the spirit land and hover near you, while you buffet the storms with your precious little freight, and wait with sad patience till we meet to part no more.

But, O Sarah! If the dead can come back to this earth and flit unseen around those they loved, I shall always be near you; in the brightest day and in the darkest night—amidst your happiest scenes and gloomiest hours—always, always; and if there be a soft breeze upon your cheek, it shall be my breath; or the cool air fans your throbbing temple, it shall be my spirit passing by.

Sarah, do not mourn me dead; think I am gone and wait for me, for we shall meet again.

As for my little boys, they will grow as I have done, and

never know a father's love and care. Little Willie is too young to remember me long, and my blue-eyed Edgar will keep my frolics with him among the dimmest memories of his childhood. Sarah, I have unlimited confidence in your maternal care and your development of their characters. Tell my two mothers his and hers I call God's blessing upon them. O Sarah, I wait for you there! Come to me, and lead thither my children.

Sullivan

My name is Dave. I learned about Steve's book from a friend and feel like I have something that matters to add to it. I love my country deliberately.

You might say that losing a leg and an eye in Vietnam when, in early 1972, a shell exploded in a truck I was riding in might testify to my love of country. Truth is I did then and I do now.

Then ... I actually enlisted because I wanted to fight for my country, to keep communism from taking over Vietnam and the rest of southeast Asia, if not eventually hitting Australia. That was what I was told and that is what I believed to be the truth. And I was not bitter about losing important parts of my body. I have never been, even with what I now know about the war ... unjust and wrong.

Now ... I would give *another* leg and eye to keep this country *out* of another unjust and wrong war. I love my country that much, that deliberately.

Madison, Wisconsin
September 2018

Fourscore and seven years ago our fathers brought forth, on this continent, a new nation, conceived in liberty, and dedicated to the proposition that all men are created equal. Now we are engaged in a great civil war, testing whether that nation, or any nation so conceived, and so dedicated, can long endure. We are met on a great battle-field of that war. We have come to dedicate a portion of that field, as a final resting-place for those who here gave their lives, that that nation might live. It is altogether fitting and proper that we should do this. But, in a larger sense, we cannot dedicate, we cannot consecrate—we cannot hallow—this ground. The brave men, living and dead, who struggled here, have consecrated it far above our poor power to add or detract. The world will little note, nor long remember what we say here, but it can never forget what they did here. It is for us the living, rather, to be dedicated here to the unfinished work which they who fought here have thus far so nobly advanced. It is rather for us to be here dedicated to the great task remaining before us—that from these honored dead we take increased devotion to that cause for which they here gave the last full measure of devotion—that we here highly resolve that these dead shall not have died in vain—that this nation, under God, shall have a new birth of freedom, and that government of the people, by the people, for the people, shall not perish from the earth.

Abraham Lincoln
Address at the Gettysburg Battlefield
19 November 1863

Part Six

Loving an Idea ... Deliberately

Only two entries in this section, yet I believe that together they speak volumes. I want to thank New Directions Publishing for granting me permission to include in this anthology my very favorite poem and the concluding piece. (It is the only selection that was not offered to me and/or was not in the public domain.) This book would have been incomplete (at least for me) without it.

Loving deliberately is being completely in the moment, utterly, totally, absolutely in the moment. It is loving Life so completely that I am able to take it all in, moment by precious moment. No distractions. I love deliberately when I am All in ... All in the moment.

Walt R.
San Francisco
2018

I Am Waiting

I am waiting for my case to come up
and I am waiting
for a rebirth of wonder
and I am waiting for someone
to really discover America
and wail
and I am waiting
for the discovery
of a new symbolic western frontier
and I am waiting
for the American Eagle
to really spread its wings
and straighten up and fly right
and I am waiting
for the Age of Anxiety
to drop dead
and I am waiting
for the war to be fought
which will make the world safe
for anarchy
and I am waiting
for the final withering away
of all governments
and I am perpetually awaiting
a rebirth of wonder

I am waiting for the Second Coming
and I am waiting
for a religious revival
to sweep thru the state of Arizona
and I am waiting

for the Grapes of Wrath to be stored
and I am waiting
for them to prove
that God is really American
and I am waiting
to see God on television
piped onto church altars
if only they can find
the right channel
to tune in on
and I am waiting
for the Last Supper to be served again
with a strange new appetizer
and I am perpetually awaiting
a rebirth of wonder

I am waiting for my number to be called
and I am waiting
for the Salvation Army to take over
and I am waiting
for the meek to be blessed
and inherit the earth
without taxes
and I am waiting
for forests and animals
to reclaim the earth as theirs
and I am waiting
for a way to be devised
to destroy all nationalisms
without killing anybody
and I am waiting
for linnets and planets to fall like rain

and I am waiting for lovers and weepers
to lie down together again
in a new rebirth of wonder

I am waiting for the Great Divide to be crossed
and I am anxiously waiting
for the secret of eternal life to be discovered
by an obscure general practitioner
and I am waiting
for the storms of life
to be over
and I am waiting
to set sail for happiness
and I am waiting
for a reconstructed Mayflower
to reach America
with its picture story and tv rights
sold in advance to the natives
and I am waiting
for the lost music to sound again
in the Lost Continent
in a new rebirth of wonder

I am waiting for the day
that maketh all things clear
and I am awaiting retribution
for what America did
to Tom Sawyer
and I am waiting
for Alice in Wonderland
to retransmit to me
her total dream of innocence

and I am waiting
for Childe Roland to come
to the final darkest tower
and I am waiting
for Aphrodite
to grow live arms
at a final disarmament conference
in a new rebirth of wonder

I am waiting
to get some intimations
of immortality
by recollecting my early childhood
and I am waiting
for the green mornings to come again
youth's dumb green fields come back again
and I am waiting
for some strains of unpremeditated art
to shake my typewriter
and I am waiting to write
the great indelible poem
and I am waiting
for the last long careless rapture
and I am perpetually waiting
for the fleeing lovers on the Grecian Urn
to catch each other up at last
and embrace
and I am awaiting
perpetually and forever
a renaissance of wonder

Lawrence Ferlinghetti

Loving an Idea ... Deliberately

Conclusion

As I worked on the organization and arrangement of the offerings in this anthology, I gave each one more good, close look. After reading only a handful, I came to the realization that this had, in fact, become two books in one. It is a collection of reflections about the term *loving deliberately*, of course. But it is something else – something that, upon further consideration, I find to be equally important: It is a collection of stories – often extraordinarily important stories – from people's *lives*. Regardless of their theme or format, they are intimate. Some are shared in a bold and open way – almost shouted out. Others are rather suggestive – like whispers to a confidant or a lover. Regardless of any differences they may have, they do have at least two characteristics in common: they are vibrant and they are so very ... *honest*.

Most of the folks – especially those whose words were created specifically for this collection – worked hard about, thought long about, and definitely struggled with what they would write and submit for inclusion. As I have stated previously, there were others – perhaps an equal number – who took on the task of contributing something for the book with equal dedication and even passion, but for many reasons were simply not able to find the words that they were comfortable with submitting. Another point I have made is that virtually everyone who took on the project – whether it resulted in something to be included or not – was thankful for having gone through the process ... in giving loving deliberately some thorough and *honest* consideration.

There is so much that I could say about what appears in the pages of this anthology and the two books in the series that preceded it. Yet, somehow, it just feels right for me to say very little more as I bring this project to a close. So many folks have already said what needs to be said. So, I will close with this comment on the theme of doing what we do – deliberately. Trying – really hard sometimes – to stay focused on what is truly important is essential, it seems to me, to living a life completely. I am talking about being in the moment, listening, seeing, thinking, feeling with a sense of urgency without feeling obliged to do so (or panicky if we aren't feeling that urgency sometimes). I would suggest that living deliberately, which is what this three-book project is and has been all about, *also* really matters to those who have participated in this project in one way or another. I would like to think that traveling, aging, loving, living deliberately is very right for just about all us – if we just take the time and make the effort to do so. It is my sincere wish that those of you who have read and thought about what this deliberately series has to offer have found within it something of real value to enrich your lives whether you have read one, two, or all three of the books. I thank you for your time and your willingness to be involved. Please ... stay in touch.

Appendix

Information letter to possible contributors to *Loving Deliberately*

January 2016 [and May 2018]

Subj: REQUEST FOR CONTRIBUTIONS TO MY BOOK: *LOVING DELIBERATELY*

Dear Contributor -

I am sending you this letter because I would like to ask you for your help with my next book, *Loving Deliberately*. Details regarding the help that I am seeking from you are found in the following paragraphs. I am sending this invitation to close friends and family members as well as people whom I do not know. As some of you may know, I am self-publishing. Consequently, I cannot pay you for your contribution, and I cannot guarantee that I will ultimately use your contribution in the final draft if you decide to submit one. I *can* guarantee that I will carefully read each contribution with great appreciation. I also guarantee that I will not edit your contribution unless it is absolutely necessary for purposes of clarity and never without your express consent. As for those of you whose contributions are included in the published draft, I will not identify you by name unless you authorize me to do so. I will send you a formal request to use the material.

Loving Deliberately is the third of my three-book series. *Traveling Deliberately* and *Aging Deliberately* are the first and second books, respectively. The central theme of all three books ("Deliberately") is directly linked to a key passage in Henry David Thoreau's great nineteenth-century work, *Walden: or, Life in the Woods:*

> I went to the woods because I wished to live deliberately, to front only the essential facts of life, and see if I could not learn what it had to teach, and not, when I came to die, discover that I had not lived….

My purpose in the series, then, is to get to the core of the meaning and importance of travel, aging, and loving . I think I had some success in accomplishing this in my first two books (specifically with the help of Dr. Tom Schneider in *Aging*). Now I am looking for the assistance of a much more vast array of contributors – one of whom, it is my hope, will be you. ***By the way, I encourage you to share this invitation with others. Their contributions are also welcome.***

What I am asking of you is to reflect on the term "loving deliberately" – not love or loving, but **loving deliberately**. I want to know what that two-word phrase means to you. Once you have thought this through, I would like you to submit a written response to me for possible inclusion in the book. The only additional guidance that I offer is a follows:

Make your response original – from *your* head, from *your* heart;

- Your response can refer to any *one* (living or dead, human or non-human) or any *thing* (a place, work, religion, travel, the sky is the limit….);

- Your response can be summed up in a brief phrase or described in a poem, anecdote, or story with a maximum length of 2000 words;
- I ask that you submit your response to me no later than thirty days from the date that you receive this invitation.

With your help, I am hoping to collect and present a wide assortment of perspectives on just what loving deliberately is about. I am also hopeful that what we will create together will be a work that people from all walks of life, all genders, all political perspectives, all spiritual views – regardless of where they are from or what they have experienced in life – can read, learn from, and grow from intellectually, emotionally, and possibly even spiritually as a result of what they have read.

Please submit your responses to me, Steve Bannow, at one of the following addresses:

Steve Bannow 1739 Mist Wood Drive Howell, MI 48843

Or

<u>stevebannow@aol.com</u>
stevenbannow@gmail.com

Every contributor – whether their contribution is included in the book or not – will receive a written acknowledgement from me along with my most sincere thanks. In any case, it is my hope that simply taking the time to reflect upon "loving deliberately" will be, in its own right, a worthwhile experience. You should also know that 50% of any profits made by the sale of this book or the set of three in the "Deliberately" series will be donated to a charitable organization to be chosen by a consensus of the published contributors. If you have questions, please feel free to call me at

>(850) 602-8485 or send me an email
>at stevebannow@aol.com.

Thank you for your consideration. I am hoping to hear from you.

Most sincerely,
Steve Bannow